Richard Thomas Wright

BARKERVILLE

Williams Creek, Cariboo

D0062409

A Gold Rush Experience

Cover photo: Barkerville, approximately one month before the Great Fire of September 1868. Photo by Richard Maynard. The man on the extreme left is Thomas Pattullo, the second man to purchase a building site in Barkerville, in 1862.

Winter Quarters Press
Box 15 Miocene, Williams Lake, B.C., Canada V2G 2P3
(250) 296-4432; fax (250) 296-4429
e-mail: rtwright@grassrootsgroup.com
http://grassrootsgroup.com

Canadian Cataloging in Publication Data

Distributed by   Sandhill Book Marketing Ltd.
                   #99 - 1270 Ellis Street
                   Kelowna, B.C., Canada V1Y 1Z4
                   (250) 763-1406; fax: (250) 763-4051

Wright, Richard Thomas   1940-
    Barkerville: A Gold Rush Experience

    Published by: Winter Quarters Press.
    First ed. had title: Discover Barkerville.
    Includes bibliographical references and index.

    ISBN 0-9696887-1-7

    1. Cariboo (B.C.: Regional district)—Gold discoveries. 2. Barkerville (B.C.)—History.   3. Barkerville (B.C.)—Guidebooks. I. Title.   II. Title: Discover Barkerville.
FC3849.B37W75 1998   971.1'75   C98-910578-4
F1089.5.B37W75 1998

Publishing history: Discover Barkerville, 1984; Barkerville: A Gold Rush Experience, 1993; revised edition, 1998; third printing, 2000.

Designed by Richard Thomas Wright
Typesetting by Cathryn Wellner
The Typeface is ITC Berkeley Oldstyle
Printed and bound in Canada by Friesen Printers, Altona, Manitoba

This book is for my sons:
Richard Thomas Wright, Jr. and Raven Carleton Wright
Thanks, guys

Three members of the 1985 Gold Escort. Photo by Louie Blanc Studio.

Acknowledgements

When I went to Barkerville in 1983 to write the first edition of this book, I was met by special people; Ken Mather, then curator; Ron Candy, conservator; and Judy Campbell, visitor services coordinator, were among them.

Ken Mather introduced me to the town and the archives and made many thoughtful and helpful suggestions and corrections. Since then he has been a wealth of knowledge and inspiration on all things to do with the gold rush. In particular he led me to the real story of Billy Barker and his roots in the fens of England as well as his early days on the Fraser.

Researcher Judy Campbell shared the Kelly House top floor with me, showed me through files, walked the town, shared wine, and when the weather turned cold, lent me her Tomato House.

Ron Candy showed me what conservation and restoration was all about. As friends we explored and got lost in some of the finest country in B.C.

Conservator Jennifer Morford told me about wallpaper and posters, the second-floor lady, and amber.

To the other residents of Kelly House, with whom I shared coffee, end-of-season parties, stories and laughter, I also owe a debt: Leah Hubensky; Ann Laing, Bert DeVink and Brian Fugler.

The Parks Branch interpreters of 1983 brought main street to life—Mike Heenan, "Big Larry" Pawlowicz, Ernie Prentice, Peter Burgis, Bill and Marilyn Rummel.

For five months I lived either in Barkerville-Wells or behind the pages of this book. Despite this, my family has always been a source of encouragement and support. I remember well climbing the stairs to my boys' bedroom one night and finding my youngest son, Raven, rereading his copy of an early book of mine, *Westering*. We sat and talked about his favorite stories—it was a special time. And I remember the many instances of encouragement and companionship provided by my oldest son, Richard. Many times he has come home and asked, "How many words today, Dad?" or "How's the book going?" I thank both my sons for their help.

All these people—Parks Branch staff, Barkerville area residents, friends and family—made this book an experience.

Richard Thomas Wright

Acknowledgements to the 1998 edition

It would not be an exaggeration to say that the first edition of this book changed my life. It introduced me to a new place and new people. Ken Mather suggested I come back the following year as an historical interpreter, to create the role of James Kelso. Those next few years introduced me to more Cariboo and gold rush history, and a wide circle of friends.

Most significant were David Karmyzyn, Dave Sayer and later Alvin Sanders. We were The Boys From Joe Denny's Saloon, playing traditional music from the gold rush era.

Recent updated versions were researched with the assistance of numerous people. Former curator Jennifer Iredale has helped with research and ideas for several years. More recently, curator Bill Quackenbush offered a place to work, access to the archives and help in seeing this 1998 edition was published.

Ken Mather continued to be a Barkerville touchstone. No fact was too obscure for his verification and no story too trivial for his interest.

Similarly the staff at the British Columbia Archives and Record Services, laboring under continued cutbacks and a loss of government support, continue to be a source of inspiration and research.

The Quesnel Genealogical Society and particularly Lana Fox's research into birth, marriages and deaths assisted research into the people of Williams Creek.

Raven Wright held our farm and ranch together while research continued and the book rewritten. Richard Jr. continues to drag toward the 21st century.

There are three special people who deserve notice:

John Premischook, an inspiration, who by simply asking me to come back to Barkerville continued a chain of events that is still unwinding.

Cathryn Wellner, my wife and best friend, who tackled Cariboo history with the enthusiasm of a convert, the ear of a storyteller and the eye of a folklorist, and who welcomed our move into the heart of Cariboo history at Pioneer Ranch.

These later editions would not have been possible without the assistance and support of the Friends of Barkerville and Cariboo Goldfields Historical Society under the presidency of the late Jerry MacDonald, who passed into history in 1998. MacDonald was one of Canada's leading editors, a mentor to dozens of journalists, a father, a friend and a strong advocate of Canadian and particularly Cariboo history.

Finally my appreciation to all those Barkervillians who make this creek come alive, both in the 19th and 20th Century; those few who labor with passion and determination, through frustration, slashed budgets and the weight of bureaucracy, to keep this piece of B.C. history alive.

Richard Thomas Wright
Pioneer Ranch
Williams Lake, B.C.
June 1998

Author's Introduction

I arrive here in the valley of Williams Creek on a sunny day cooled by clouds that hang over the Cariboo Mountains. A breeze rustles down the creek, shimmering the cottonwoods, quaking the aspens. The town is bustling, for this day marks the end of a depressing wet period. The warm air has dried the street so I can walk the roadway rather than the boardwalk that fronts the buildings.

Ahead, a woman's skirt sweeps the street and raises little clouds of dust. Up the Valley of Flags I walk, past St. Saviour's Anglican Church, past Overlander John Bowron's house, the tinshop, the blacksmith's shop. The sweet smells of sourdough waft from the bakery, and a squirrel bounces across the street with a pecan nut—stolen from Mason & Daly's General Store. "Dr. Carroll" strolls the boardwalk talking to visitors, and the summer minister, dressed in black tunic, skirt and hat and swinging his walking stick, stops to say hello. "Mr. Mason," merchant, tips his hat and a bonneted lady smiles.

At the Wake-Up Jake Cafe I climb onto the boardwalk, think of bannock and coffee, and then cut between the buildings toward the back street and Kelly House, 20th-century offices of this 19th-century town. The desk graciously provided is on the top floor. With little effort I become part of 1870; the problem lies in returning to the present.

It was about 20 years ago that I first visited Barkerville, soon after it was designated a provincial park. Since then I have traveled the gold rush country often, caught up as the prospectors were 100 years ago. The prospectors, you see, unlike the miners, did not really go for the gold, but for the going. I did likewise.

The first edition of this book came out of those traveling years and several concentrated months of research and writing. This second edition is influenced by several years as James Kelso, Overlander, a historical interpreter in Barkerville, and more years of research. It attempts to tell not only the story of Barkerville but of the men and women who lived along Williams Creek. In particular, I have enjoyed telling the stories of little-known people: the miners who worked for wages, the dance hall girls, the Chinese shopkeepers, the men who died here or went home broke. For while the Camerons and Barkers and Begbies are significant, they did not exist in a vacuum. The aristocrat and the newly-made millionaire lived and worked beside the unsung, dirty digger.

There is a danger in working on a book such as this. "Research is endlessly seductive," historian Barbara Tuchman says. I concur. Names from miners' records and store ledgers have frequently taken on lives and stories of their own. My regret is that not all the stories can be told in this book. But I cannot rebury these individuals, and if one is your long-sought-after great-grandfather, I would welcome hearing from you and exchanging information. I can be contacted through the co-publisher, Winter Quarters Press.

A suggestion to those who travel to Barkerville. While I was there a man walked into the museum's visitor center, had a quick look around and said, "Is this all there is?" A site interpreter explained that, no, there was a whole town just up the road. But there is even more than the town itself. If you travel to Barkerville allow yourself time to walk the roads, hike the trails and talk to the interpreters. Soon Barkerville of long ago will come alive.

I hope this book brings you as much pleasure as I experienced researching and writing it. Enjoy these stories, and then go and find more.

Richard Thomas Wright

Note: A few years ago, Canada went metric. The conversion has often made the interpretation of historic measurements complicated and written history jarring. In an effort to make this guide easily understood and useful to the reader, the editor decided to use both the Imperial and metric systems in the most logical manner possible. Therefore, in the modern-day travel guide sections of this book, for example "The Road to the Gold Creeks," the metric system of measure is used. In the other sections of the book, for example "The Walking Tour," all measures are Imperial.

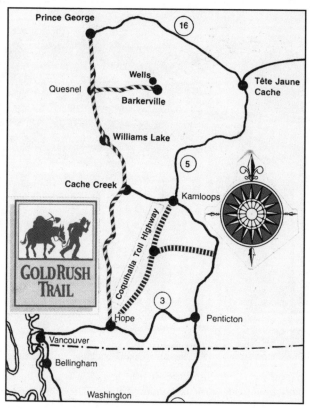

Barkerville Hotel in 1894. Standing on the boardwalk are: fourth from left, John Knott and sixth from left, John Hauser. The Barkerville Hotel now houses the Root Beer Saloon. PABC #10084

CONTENTS

THE RUSH FOR GOLD

An introduction to Williams Creek

Sunday, April 25, 1858, Victoria, Vancouver's Island.

The small community based around the Hudson's Bay Company's fur trading post, Fort Victoria, is preparing for the Sabbath. They are on their way to church when an unexpected steamer pulls into the tight harbour. It is the *Commodore* out of San Francisco. Not far behind are the *Golden Age,* the *Stockholm* and the *Columbia.* They disembark 1700 gold seekers into a population of less than 300 white settlers. During the summer the fort is surrounded by over 6000 tents, and by the time the leaves turn there is a permanent Victoria population of over 3000. Over 30,000 men and women arrive in B.C. that summer. The fur trade economy is yanked into the 19th century.

"Gold! Gold on Fraser's River." The news spread down the Pacific coast from port to port, swelling like an ocean wave until it washed into San Francisco Bay. Rumor described miners washing a month's wages of $25 in a day, and even Indian women were said to be panning $10 a day.

"Where is Fraser's River?" According to miner Thomas Seward, no one knew, but word of a new strike hitting a depressed gold-based region "was enough to send hundreds of men into the wilderness to make their fortunes or to die in the attempt."

Fraser's River was, they soon found, north—in British Territory. Most miners "did not even know that Great Britain had possessions on the Pacific Coast." But they eventually found Fraser's River and came by the thousands, an immense rush that emptied San Francisco. On April 20, 1858, an estimated 1700 men left between 4:00 and 5:30 p.m. Montgomery Street "looked as deserted as on a Sabbath Day." The new El Dorado was north. The rush for Fraser's River was on.

The North American search for the Goddess of Dawn, the Gilded One, gold, had begun before Spanish *conquistadores* rode roughshod over the native population in search of the Seven Cities of Gold. The discovery had to wait three centuries, until 1847, when James Marshall found gold in the tail-race of a mill he was building for self-styled feudal lord John Sutter. By the end of 1848, 10,000 men scratched for gold in the Sierra Nevadas. The following year the '49ers streamed west, over land and sea, until the creeks and rivers overflowed with gold diggers. In this rush there were men from Canada: James Wattie, John A. Cameron and others who would later become legends in the Cariboo rush. The gold recovery was enormous. On the Feather River, for instance, seven miners panned 275 pounds of gold in two weeks.

As men continued to pour into California and deplete the gold, they spread out east and north, over the next mountain. There was gold

The Rankin Tunnel, a good gold producer. PABC #10161

in Ballarat, Australia, in 1851. Many followed that rush; then the Queen Charlotte Islands gave false hopes in 1852. By now the population of California was over 250,000. Many were miners waiting impatiently for any hint of a new strike. Only a whisper was needed, because when gold was there you had to rush, you had to be first.

Prospectors following wisps of reports had made their way into British Territory north of the 49th parallel by the early 1850s. Gold had been found on the Columbia River near Fort Colville, on the Similkameen River, and on the Thompson River near Fort Kamloops. Hudson's Bay Company men ignored the gold until Governor James Douglas at Fort Victoria heard of the finds and told them, "Acquire all the gold you can."

This "discovery of much importance," as Douglas called it, brought the fur trade era to an end in New Caledonia and entered the colony into the gold era. To say Hudson's Bay Company (HBC) entered this new era with reluctance is an understatement. The vast wilderness known as Rupert's Land and New Caledonia had been controlled for 200 years by the HBC as the "true and absolute Lordes and Proprietors." They held a trade monopoly from the Canadian Shield to the Pacific Ocean and thereby ruled the population. This monopoly was based on the fur trade; any shift toward gold mining, settlement and agriculture would upset the delicate scales on which their profitable trade balanced.

It was with mixed emotions that James Douglas instructed his traders to accept gold. He anticipated that word would soon leak out and American miners would pour across the border, necessitating the establishment of British sovereignty over gold claims. There was no legislative body and no person of authority other than himself. To protect British territory, Douglas assumed that role.

On December 28, 1857, Douglas issued a proclamation stating that all gold mines on the Fraser and Thompson rivers belonged to the British Crown. Basing his actions on the Australian experience, he announced a system of mining licences, the fee to be 10 shillings or $5 American. Anyone removing gold from the district without having been authorized would "be prosecuted, both criminally and civilly, as the law allows."

Barkerville in 1865. Note the pack saddles on the horses and the carcasses on the porch. Charles Gentile photo. PABC #95328

With these precautions taken, Douglas gathered 800 ounces of gold from his forts and shipped it south to the San Francisco mint on the *S.S. Otter.* The word was out and the rush was on.

The first wave came from the west coast; a second came as news reached the eastern seaboard. After initial hesitation, newspapers accepted the stories and the British Colonial Office in London, England, realized that perhaps these gold finds were more important than previously imagined. Officials knew they must pay some attention to this discovery, for while the 1846 Treaty of Washington had set the boundary at the forty-ninth parallel, it had not stopped the expansionist designs of some Americans. The west coast, sparsely populated, unorganized and unprotected, was threatened by foreign immigration and American "sovereignty by occupation" claims.

The reaction of the new Colonial Secretary, Sir Edward Bulwer Lytton, was to present a bill to Parliament that would make New Caledonia a crown colony. Lytton's move was not solely a response to the tide of American miners nor a result of his unbounded faith in the new colony's riches. Instead Lytton saw his bill as a way to open free trade by ending the HBC monopoly. The bill was read July 1, 1858, and a week later a temporary five-year plan for government was added. Before royal assent, the name of the colony was changed to British Columbia, which, in Queen Victoria's opinion, was "the best name."

The bill approved on August 2, 1858, created two colonies—British Columbia and Vancouver Island. James Douglas, after 37 years with HBC, accepted governorship of the two colonies. Immediately, a detachment of 150 Royal Engineers under Colonel Richard Moody was dispatched from England to survey land for public sale, lay out the capital, construct roads and assist the governor in any way possible.

The gold rush that had created the new colonies turned into a "humbug" for some as the high waters of spring drowned the gold-bearing sandbars. While thousands retreated to California, many more squatted on the Fraser's banks ready for further digging. The Fraser's fine gold led Californian and Australian miners to believe that upstream there would be streams with coarse gold and, perhaps, the mother lode. Scattered along the river were California miners such as William Downie, Ned Stout, Billy Barker, Dutch Bill Dietz, Doc Keithley, Richard Willoughby, John Cameron and Peter Dunleavy.

Not all miners waited on the Fraser. As early as 1858 Aaron Post was recorded at the mouth of the Chilcotin River. Then in the spring of 1859 Peter Dunleavy camped here. A Shuswap Indian named Tomah stopped for tea and in return told them his cousin Long Bacheese (Baptiste) would lead them to bean-sized nuggets of gold. True to his word, Baptiste later led the miners to Horsefly River and the promised nuggets. His trail was still warm when the Neil Campbell party arrived, announcing that there were hundreds of miners hard on their heels. So began the rush for "Cariboo," a corruption of the name of the deerlike mammal *cariboeuf* or caribou that roamed the alpine meadows of the region.

Meanwhile a second approach was being made to Cariboo, this time via the Quesnel River, by Benjamin MacDonald, a Prince Edward Islander. Prospecting out of Fort Alexandria on the Fraser, MacDonald found his first gold on the "Canal River" in June 1859.

In response to the Dunleavy and MacDonald strikes, a multitude of streams were being prospected. By 1860 the town of Quesnelle Forks had blossomed where the Quesnel and Cariboo rivers meet. Restless prospectors pushed further east and north.

Only two years earlier most California miners had not known there were British possessions in the north and certainly had never heard of Fraser's River. Now a new river was being mined, fully 350 miles north of the border. The region was as remote as anything imagined by the miners, a country known only to natives and fur trappers. "It seemed as difficult of access as the Arctic regions," one miner wrote.

Doc Keithley and his partner I.P. Diller made a good strike above Cariboo Lake on a creek later called Keithley. By the time the best claims were struck a year later, a town called Keithley Creek was in full swing. Doc Keithley, George Weaver, John Rose and Benjamin MacDonald were hiking north again. From a high plateau they looked across alpine meadows sparkling in the autumn sun and saw creeks flowing north. Choosing one creek the men made their way downstream, through a pass into a canyon. They found gold lying exposed—"sun-burn gold" that had begun to oxidize. From one pan

Oldtimers of Barkerville.

they cleared $75, from another $100. They continued to prospect, staked the best land they could find, built a cabin and then headed back to Keithley Creek for supplies.

Despite their efforts to "blind" their trail when they left Keithley to cross the Snowshoe Plateau—now covered in several feet of snow—they were followed by Cariboo miners. At the new creek, named Antler for the deer antlers along the banks, 1200 miners were at work in the spring of 1861. By July the canyon town had 60 houses and the miners' wealth had brought in racehorses, theatrical troupes, women and dozens of whiskey mills. Antler was a strike to write home about, and newspapers had a headline heyday. The *Colonist* of Victoria: "LATER FROM CARIBOO! New Diggings—Great Excitement. $75 TO THE PAN!" Anyone who had doubts about Cariboo's wealth was now convinced that here indeed was the road to riches.

The Antler strikes drew headlines in the eastern press and once again lured men west. They came by sea, they came north through the U.S., and they came overland across the plains and prairies.

Taken in the early 1900s. PABC #C10108

Dutch Bill Dietz was an Antler Creek latecomer. Luck had not been with him in this gold rush. His journey from California had netted him only a little Fraser River gold and a lot of trouble from Indians who stole his supplies at Lillooet. Now he was late arriving at the Antler strike. With several miners he headed up Antler Creek, across the broad alpine plateau called Bald Mountain and down into another watershed.

Work at the new creek found by the Dutch Bill party was slow, for they had brought only one pick. As night came on they stopped to build a fire and cook dinner. Later, while the others sat by the fire, Dutch Bill scouted around. From a high ledge he took a pan of gravel, thawed it in the stream and, with aching hands, washed it out. There was $1 in gold in the pan. He panned again, and again. As darkness came he headed back to his companions. They were not impressed with the find but agreed to name the creek for Dutch Bill after he promised, "if you vill call it by me, I vill hoppen for you de very first case of vine vot comes into de country." It was an offer too good to

15

refuse, and "William's Creek" it was.

The transformation this post-glacial creek underwent from its 1861 discovery until 1863 was explosive. Word of the Williams Creek strike soon reached Antler. Dissatisfied miners raced over Bald Mountain and past the headwaters of the creek to a place where the water narrowed at a small canyon. While initial enthusiasm was high, the gold of Williams Creek did not give itself up easily. Miners who expected the easy diggings of Antler Creek dubbed it Humbug Creek. The diggings went down to a layer of hard blue clay that miners thought was bedrock and on which most of the gold was found. Returns were mediocre.

At Abbott's and Jourdan's claim frustration was intense. Jourdan left for supplies, and Abbott decided to swing a few blows at the blue clay. Abbott's pick broke through, and when Jourdan returned he had 50 ounces of nuggets to show. No longer was this "Humbug Creek." Over the hill, Richard Willoughby found gold on what he dubbed Lowhee Creek. A few miles away, claims were staked on Lightning Creek. The rush was really on.

Only 90 men and seven women stayed on the creek during the winter of 1861-62; the rest went south and spread word of the strikes. Abbott assisted by scattering gold through Victoria's saloons. The gold sent to Victoria as winter fell on Cariboo was recorded at $2,600,000. Few could resist the lure of gold shipments or the temptation to shoulder a shovel and head north.

Dear Joe, I am well and so are the rest of the boys. I avail myself of the present opportunity to write you a half dozen lines to let you know I am well, and doing well—making from two to three thousand dollars a day! Times good—grub high—whiskey bad—money plenty.

Yours truly, William Cunningham.

Bill Cunningham announced spring's arrival on the creeks with this letter on May 18, 1862. As he wrote, the trails crawled with men. On Lightning Creek a town called Van Winkle was already in existence, and on Williams Creek Richfield was taking shape—cabins first, then saloons.

Downstream from Richfield was a small canyon. The claims below that gave little sign of being productive. Then Ned Stout and some partners tried a tributary gulch. They called it Stout's Gulch when the party found gold and began bringing in $1000 a day. Stout's strike proved there was gold below the canyon.

One man who recognized the canyon's potential was an English riverman who had been scratching for gold since he first reached North America around 1846. William Barker had arrived on Williams Creek early in the spring of 1861 and had a claim near Mink Gulch, above Richfield. The claim was unsuccessful. Early the next summer, June 1862, Barker moved downstream.

At the downstream claim Barker and company, now expanded to eight partners and claims, sank two shafts with no success. They began again and on August 17, 1862, hit the lead. In the next ten hours they took out 124 ounces of gold.

Quesnelle Forks was the first town of significance in Cariboo. When this photo by J.H. Blume was taken in 1899, the town's population was 98 percent Chinese. VCA

Gold Commissioner Thomas Elwyn wrote the Colonial Secretary that he considered this strike "to be of great importance for now the lead will in all probability be traced for a long distance down the creek." Elwyn was right on the mark. Claims, shaft houses, flumes, water wheels and cabins sprouted along the creek like fireweed after a fire. And four months later John Angus "Cariboo" Cameron, another Fraser River miner, struck rich gravel just a mile below Barker & Co.

By spring of 1863 two towns had grown, with these two claims as their center. With Richfield upstream and Cameronton downstream the obvious name was Middletown. But that did not stick. Nor did Springfield, for the hillside springs, nor Vandoulanville, after miner Charles Vandoulan or even Williams Creek. It was Barkerville.

Everywhere the earth was being turned inside out for its wealth. By 1864 there were four towns in four miles on Williams Creek. Richfield, the "seat of Government," was furthest upstream. Below the canyon were Barkerville and Cameronton, forming one long main street of hotels, saloons, brothels, general stores, restaurants and numerous less important buildings. Little mention is made of Marysville, but Fred Ludditt says the town was scattered on the flats below Cameronton and on the benches of the creek's east side. Nearby were the rich Forest Rose and California claims and Adam's sawmill.

The gold towns along Williams Creek went through three phases: the Discovery Phase of 1860-63, when individual miners prospected their way north and mined with the simplest of methods; the Mature Phase of 1864-78, when more sophisticated shaft and tunnel mining techniques removed deep placer deposits; and the Hydraulic Mining Phase of 1879-85, when shaft and tunnel mining declined and the emphasis shifted to large-scale, heavily capitalized hydraulic mining

The Mucho Oro Claim was located near the mouth of Stout's Gulch. It was a low producer with only $50,000 reported produced by 1896. VPL #8640

that left the hills and valleys laced with water systems. It was during the Mature Phase that long-term operations financed by companies of men were the norm. The stability of these operations and the completion of the Cariboo Road in 1865 provided the opportunity to use better technology and created a base for merchants.

While gold held out and miners' riches filled merchants' tills, the area prospered. But soon there was not enough business for all four towns. Marysville faded early on, then Cameronton and Richfield—although for years the government tenaciously hung onto its offices and court house. The face of the creek changed radically in 1868 when most of Barkerville burned down, to be replaced by a less crowded, more orderly townsite. This new town likely played a part in the demise of the surrounding towns.

By the late 1880s what remained of Cameronton had merged with Barkerville, which, as times became tough, emerged as the permanent town on Williams Creek. Even at that, Barkerville's life ebbed. Strikes on Lightning Creek drew miners away. As the gold that opened the country dwindled, men drifted to other towns, to pioneer ranches, to home in the east or to the coast. A few stayed to wash huge hydraulic pits or tunnel into the mountain. They kept some life in the old town.

With its heyday past, Barkerville slipped into relative obscurity at the turn of the century, then surged briefly to life again when a second wave of miners came looking for wages in the 1929-39 Depression years. World War II ended the brief revival and pushed Barkerville toward ghost town status.

Fortunately, the historic value of Williams Creek in general and

The historical interpreters of Barkerville bring life to the restored town, becoming miners, merchants, tradesmen of the 1870s. Ronald Candy photo.

Barkerville in particular was pointed out to the government by a few remaining residents, such as Fred Ludditt, and the Cariboo Historical Society during the 1950s. As B.C.'s centennial year approached a young MLA for Cariboo, Bill Speare, gave his maiden speech in the house. He spoke of Barkerville and Cariboo's history. Premier W.A.C. Bennett seized on Speare's dream as a focus for the 1958 centennial, and Barkerville was declared a historic park.

The purpose of the park, as described in the 1958 Master Plan, is to "preserve, present and manage for public benefit the historic town and representative or significant elements of historical value related to the Cariboo Gold Rush." The site, now referred to as Barkerville Historic Townsite, is to be developed as a museum of the 1858 to 1885 period. Since the fire of 1868 destroyed most of Barkerville, the buildings, the goods, the services and the park's other interpretive materials focus primarily on 1870. However, the town cannot be seen in this 1800s context alone, for it continued to live, through the quiet, turn-of-the-century years into the hard-rock boom years of the 1930s and beyond. As building continued so does the interpretation of this historic townsite, with some displays representing the 1890s and the 1930s.

Thus the gold that was a catalyst in the creation of the colony and then the province of British Columbia also created Barkerville. Old camps and townsites have decayed beneath second growth forests and hydraulic mining tailings. Today, Barkerville Historic Townsite stands as sole representative of that time: "The days of old, the days of gold."

GOLD RUSH SOCIETY

The Miners - Winners and Losers

Restored Barkerville illustrates not only a time and a place but a society. Walking down the main street you might imagine that all the people in Barkerville were merchants, but merchants were in the minority. The majority were miners, always hard at work, often poor and unhealthy. Debt chained men to the creeks. Without money they could not leave, and there was always the chance the next shovelful would bring gold or the next claim pay better wages.

The Sheepshead Claim, Williams Creek, 1867-68. PAC #C19423

Williams Creek often yielded its gold in immensely rich pockets. For example: from 120 feet of ground, the Steel Company took $120,000; from 500 feet the Cunningham Company took $270,000; from 50 feet the Diller Company took $240,000 and from 80 feet the Burns Company took $140,000—at a time when the average wage in eastern Canada was $1 a day, and on Williams Creek $4-10 a day.

Far more common were the men who came to Cariboo poor and desperate, and left destitute and despairing. Mining was difficult. If you arrived on a crowded creek too late, the ground was staked and you had to buy a claim or shares with any available capital. Otherwise, you earned a living by working for another company in a deep, cold, wet shaft. If your claim did prove up, it was difficult to work on your own. To raise money for equipment and labor, you had to sell shares, and the profits, if any, would be divided. More often, a man went home wiser rather than wealthy. And there were those who stayed in the cemetery on the hill.

Details of a miner's hard life are recorded in the letters of Robert Harkness, an Overlander of '62. Writing to his wife Sabrina, Harkness speaks of two things—his love for her and his day-to-day struggle.

Richfield, June 10, 1863...You must pay well for everything you get here. Flour is $1.12 a pound. This is at the rate of $225 per barrel. Beans & rice are each a dollar a pound. Sugar is $1.75, nails $2, Tea (very poor) $3, Tobacco $5. It may seem extravagant to pay $5 a pound for tobacco but I do like to sit & smoke & think of my far away Nina. Salt is $1.25 a pound, equal to $17.50 for such a little sack as we used to sell for ninepence. Potatoes are $1.25 a pound or $75 a bushel. A clay pipe or a box of matches, such as we get at home for a copper, costs half a dollar here.

Robert Harkness, Overlander

Gilbert Munro, Aus McIntosh & I came up together & we still live in a brush tent together. Munro was lucky enough to get work the first day he came at making shingles & has been at work every day since. Aus has not had work to do. I have been working at whatever I could get to do but have not got steady work. I expect to go to work for the Brouses next week & work steadily. As soon as I can save a couple of hundred dollars I'll send them home to you. Wages are ten dollars a day, out of which you must, of course, board yourself. We live on bread, beans & bacon, with an occasional mess of very tough beef ($0.50 a pound) & manage to subsist for from three to four dollars a day each. ...I worked pretty hard today carrying stones to a man building a chimney. ...

Williams Creek, May 31, 1864. My own darling wife...Very many have left & are leaving every day, unable to earn enough to procure grub. I am very comfortable compared to what I was last summer. For two summers past, I have been "pitching my tents" but this year I have a good cabin to live in. ...There are two other men living in the same cabin but each cooks & eats by himself.

Williams Creek, June 28, 1864. I worked for the "Bed Rock Drain Co." up to last Saturday, but had to take all my pay in stock, except about 60 dollars. The stock is unsalable now, money is very scarce, work hard to get and times dull. I am doing nothing at present but hope to get work again soon. ...Charley Bowen is still on Lowhee Creek, prospects of getting anything there not very brilliant. Josh Bowen & Aus McIntosh are both working in the Montreal claim. Gilbert Munro has been making shakes but is not likely to do so well this summer as last.

Harkness and his friends wintered in New Westminster doing odd jobs, returning to Barkerville each spring to try again. In his last letter from New Westminster, in the spring of 1865 (he returned home the following year), he has turned pessimist and says, "Gilbert Munro intends starting direct for Cariboo in a few days. He persists in thinking there may be 'luck' for him in the mines, but I consider it is a matter of serious doubt whether he ever gets home at all or not." [Monroe was still here in the 1890s.]

Another pessimist, Alexander Allan, owner of the *Cariboo Sentinel*, wrote home after selling his business in 1868:

There are, it is true, many who have made and are now making their fortunes, but it is also too true here that the far greater number rank as unfortunates, those whose lot...is worse than the most miserable and poverty-stricken person in the Old Country—many of these poor fellows brought up in luxury and wealth have to live in hovels here of a description even worse than the barns into which beggars used to be put in old times—and this too in a climate where the mercury freezes (which it did, not 3 weeks ago) and they often have to go to their laborious toil (pursued in holes where they are continually drenched to the skin with water) with but scantily filled stomachs.

Disenchanted miner William Mark wrote a bitter letter in 1862 to Donald Fraser, who had been promoting Cariboo in the Victoria *Times* newspaper.

There had been a great deal said about the richness of this creek [Antler Creek] and the quantity of gold taken out from time to time; but not a word was said on the other side of the question, and there had been several companies ruined at this creek. One company, a party of eight Cornishmen...were on ground adjoining this rich claim. We passed and repassed the place for many days. They took up eight claims, one hundred square feet to a claim. They had worked for months, had diverted the river, put in flumes, prepared their sluice boxes, got their pumps and all other necessary apparatus ready for work, and yet they never struck it in sufficient quantities to pay for working. The day we left Antler they abandoned the place, and left it ruined men. This was the case with every other creek; some struck it rich, and this was blazed in every paper. The many lost all they had, and were completely beggared. This was never named but hushed down.

William Barker

There are numerous myths associated with the Cariboo gold rush: Barkerville's being the "largest city north of San Francisco"; few women on the creeks; a crimeless gold rush society; Moses' solving Blessing's murder by recognizing a hurdy's gold nugget, which he did not; and many others. But perhaps the greatest myth was the story of Billy Barker, one that began at the time of his death. It said Barker was a Cornishman, a potter by trade, a British Naval deserter who jumped ship in Victoria to follow the Fraser rush, who married when he struck it rich and whose wife ran off when he ran out of money. The crack in this legend came in 1984 when Barkerville curator Ken Mather discovered the true story: that Barker was a riverman from Cambridgeshire who left a family in England and reached North

Billy Barker

America around the time of the California gold rush; that he had continued mining all his life; that his wife had died, not run off. The rest of the story was filled in by various researchers, to give a profile of this gold rush pioneer.

When Billy Barker and his company struck the lead on Williams Creek in August 1862, he was 45 years old. In terms of the era's life expectancy, he was on his way to old age. This strike was the culmination of years of prospecting and mining.

Baptized June 7, 1817, in March, Cambridgeshire, William was the sixth child and fourth son of Samuel and Jane Barker. Samuel was a waterman, and William naturally followed in his father's wake.

In his 21st summer William met Jane Lavender, a 27-year-old widow. She had led a hard life. At 18 she had a child out of wedlock; the following year she married boatwright Robert Lavender; six months later she had a child who only lived four months. Four children followed, but when the last child was only a few months old her husband Robert died, April 1839. He was a pub keeper at the time. Two weeks later her father died. Jane was likely desperate, perhaps destitute. There was no welfare safety net.

Jane may have met William Barker when he stopped at her husband's pub; if not they met quickly, for in August 1839 they conceived a child. They married in October, at Bluntisham cum Earith, an inland port for barges.

Emma Eliza (named for William's sister) was born May 3, 1840. A year later Barker's father died. Changes were in the wind. The railway boom portended change, and by 1850 the Great Northern Railway had knocked the bottom out of barge freighting. Sometime

23

between 1842 and 1846 William Barker left the fens of England and came to North America.

Barker's early years in America are a blank. There were many William Barkers who emigrated, and his trail is cold. But he did mine in the California rush. In the meantime his wife and daughter were in the Doddington, Cambridgeshire, Union Workhouse. His wife died there on May 25, 1850, of secondary syphilis. His daughter Emma stayed in the workhouse.

Barker was on the Fraser by the second mining season. He and partner John Butson were issued licences on September 29, 1859, at Lillooet. He and some other California miners were working on Canada Bar and dealing in water rights from nearby creeks. Here he met Bishop George Hills, who recorded the meeting in his journal, which Ken Mather read 125 years later. He had not contacted his family for 14 years, he said, since his daughter was two. He promised Hill he would.

By the time Barker came to Williams Creek, he was an irascible 44-year-old with the appearance of having been hit on the head with a large mallet. He was short, about five foot nothing, heavily built with slightly bowed legs, a bushy graying beard and an easily inflamed temper. Barker arrived early in the spring of 1861 and with five other men staked the Barker & Co. claim near Mink Gulch, above Richfield, next to Major William Downie's claim. The claim was unsuccessful. Early the next summer, June 1862, Barker moved downstream and in partnership with four other Englishmen staked a second claim, contrary to the Mining Act. Barker was thus forced to sell his shares in the upper claim, just before it began producing.

At the downstream claim Barker and company, now expanded to eight claims, sank two shafts with no success. They began again and on August 17, 1862, at 40 feet rich gravel was struck. In the next ten hours they took out 124 ounces of gold. They valued their share at $20,000 each.

Anglican Bishop Hills wrote, "Head of the lead having been struck on Barker's claim...all for some days after having been 'on the Spree' that is more or less intoxicated & off work, excepting one...a very worthy young Englishman & well brought up." The one Englishman well brought up appears to be Charles Hankin, the only member to overwinter and caretake the claim. A story circulated that Judge Begbie financed the Barker Company. In fact Begbie, through a man named Walker, invested after the strike, an extreme example of conflict of interest. Begbie did not admit to the deal for many years, though newspapers editorialized over the rumored breach of conduct.

Here again Barker met Bishop Hills and told him he had contacted his family and was considering returning home. Gold was burning a hole in Billy's pocket. He and six partners headed for Victoria. Within a couple of months, on January 13, 1863, he married another widow, Elizabeth Collyer, who had arrived on the ship *Rosedale*. Elizabeth and Billy partied the winter away then headed back to Barkerville in the spring. The claim was worked continuously, with three shafts and a Cornish wheel going full tilt. Barker left at the end of the summer with even more money.

Windlass at the Barker Claim. The man second from left is thought to be Billy Barker. PAC #C19424

When he returned in the summer of 1864, the claim was not producing the way it had and by July he had sold all his interest. In total Barker had likely taken in close to $500,000 in today's money. It appears that by the end of the summer of 1864, he may have been broke. Not only did he sell out his interest in the claim but he defaulted on a loan to Robert Burnaby and Edward Henderson and gave them land he held as security for a loan to William Winnard, the Barkerville blacksmith who was facing bankruptcy.

In May 1865 Elizabeth left him. She died in Victoria. Barker wrote again to his daughter.

Barker's money was certainly invested, at least in part, in other mining ventures. He was a partner in the Never Miss Co. in 1864 and 65 and by the late 60s was working at a claim called Barker No. 2 on Valley Creek. In 1873 he led a prospecting expedition to the Horsefly country and continued working there through the 1870s. Billy's last hurrah was a claim on Donovan or Poor Man's Creek near Beave Pass. It was a partnership of old prospectors, all of whom would die the next decade.

Barker often wintered in Clinton where several of his old partn had settled on ranches: John Chenhall, John Butson, John Pollard, J Westley and Robert Walker. It was there that his friends suggeste go to Victoria and have a cancer on his jaw attended to. In Ja 1894 he went to the Old Men's Home in Victoria, but doctors fou cancer too far advanced to operate. Billy Barker, Cambrid waterman and Cariboo miner, died July 11, 1894. He was 77 yea

John Angus "Cariboo" Cameron

John A. Cameron, nicknamed "Cariboo" Cameron, was descended from a long line of stalwart Scots who came to British America in 1745. Cameron was raised on the family farm near Cornwall, Canada West, the United Empire Loyalist settlement to which his family retreated during the American War of Independence. In 1852 Cameron headed for the gold fields of California, then in 1858 he and two brothers went north to the Fraser gold rush. From the two strikes Cameron made $20,000 and returned to his home in Cornwall to marry his childhood sweetheart, Sophia Groves, a farmer's daughter 12 years his junior. Soon after the wedding, news of the immense goldfields of Cariboo filtered east and John, Sophia and their one-year-old daughter, Alice, headed west again by way of Panama.

John Angus "Cariboo" Cameron

The Camerons arrived in Victoria on February 27, 1862, after a long trip that weakened the child. Robert Stevenson claims he met his old friend Cameron in Victoria and helped him get his supplies on credit. (Mining records indicate the two friends are more likely to have met on Williams Creek.) However, before John and Sophia could leave the coast 14-month-old Alice died. Saddened but determined, John and Sophia Cameron headed north to Antler Creek and then over Bald Mountain to Williams Creek where they staked their claims.

Cameron had, like Billy Barker, staked claims on the upper part of Williams Creek but was attracted downstream by Ned Stout's success. A company was formed of John and Sophia Cameron, Allan McDonald, Richard Rivers, and Charles and James Clendennin. Three ʼeks later a claim owned by Robert Stevenson was added, but after a ʼk he transferred all his interests to Sophia Cameron. Years later ʼson said he and Cameron had quarrelled over the location of the Cameron wanted single claims on the left (west) bank of the ʼalf-mile or so below the Barker shaft, and Stevenson wanted ʼvo, abreast, on the right bank. Cameron won and it was ʼameron Claim.

ʼ did not pay off quickly, and as the winter of 1863 miners began to wonder if this was the right location. ʼt the only concern. Typhoid was raging along the ʼns had another child, but it was stillborn. Then ʼid. There was a doctor on the creek who tried to ʼa difficult, complaining patient. On October 22, ʼpped to -34 degrees C, Sophia died. Cameron ʼed to carry out her last wish and bury her at ʼ, away from the tragic creek. Her body was

25

placed in a tin casket in a wooden coffin and buried temporarily beneath a deserted cabin. There had been 5000 miners on the creek during the summer—only 90 men and seven women remained to attend Sophia Cameron's winter funeral.

The digging was hard. The first shaft failed and with the onslaught of a heavy snowfall the Clendennins had abandoned the claim and joined the migration of miners heading south for Victoria. The rest of the partners continued to dig, then hired Overlander of '62 William Halpenny and several others to help.

Two months after Sophia's death, on December 22, 1862, Stevenson and Halpenny struck gold; Santa Claus had arrived early. Bedrock was struck at 38 feet but the richest gravel was at 22 feet. The claim was rich enough that by the end of January a grieving but wealthy Cameron offered $12 a day and a $2000 bonus at Victoria to any miner who would help him haul out Sophia's coffin. Twenty-two men started out, several turning back at each roadhouse until only Cameron, Stevenson, Dr. Wilkinson, A. Rivers, Rosser Edwards, Evan Jones, French Joe and Big Indian Jim were left. Eventually they left the snow behind, and Cameron and Stevenson bought a horse and continued on on their own to Port Douglas and by steamer to Victoria.

The difficulty of hauling the coffin (and by some accounts 50 pounds of gold) through winter snow is an indication of Cameron's dedication and determination. Sophia was buried in Victoria in March, 1863. Yet Cameron had not forsaken business. In Victoria he bought out the Clendennins and two adjacent claims, giving him five full shares of the company, then headed back to his claims.

The Cameron company mined vigorously throughout the summer of 1863 while the new town of Cameronton grew up around the claims. In July Cameron was hiring as many men as he could: 60 were at work and it was expected to rise to 150. Three shafts were producing. The gold was pouring out not in ounces but in pansful.

And to top off his wealth, the burgeoning town was named for him, Cameron Town.

In autumn Cameron went south again, ready to fulfill his promise to Sophia. He took $300,000 in gold and shares that would later net him another $40,000, a total of over $5 million in today's dollars. He sold most of his shares but hung on to one interest until 1866.

At home in Canada West, Cameron's money was gratefully received by a number of beneficiaries. Three brothers got $20,000 each, and the two brothers who had been with Cameron in Cariboo got $40,000 and a farm each. Cameron married Christianne Wood in 1865 and made investments in timber, the construction of the Lachine Canal and even some eastern mines. The investments were not as successful as the Cameron company on Williams Creek.

Meanwhile, rumors rumbled. Why had Cameron taken the trouble to bring Sophia's body home? She had been sold into slavery— the coffin was filled with gold, they said. No one could accept that Cameron had simply, but with difficulty, fulfilled the dying wish of the woman he loved. When a New York paper reported Sophia's returning from slavery in an Indian tribe to Cameron's new Cornwall mansion, the infuriated man reluctantly agreed to exhume his wife's body and end speculation. The coffin was raised, and surrounded by family, friends and the curious, John A. "Cariboo" Cameron poured out the alcohol that had preserved young Sophia. Sophia was identified, the casket was closed and the rumors were laid to rest. And grass never grew again where the alcohol had drained.

"Cariboo" Cameron did return to the goldfields. In 1886, his fortune reduced, he and his second wife made another try for the gold, but it was too late. The easy-to-reach gold he had known was gone, and he was an old man. Soon after he arrived in Barkerville, he suffered a massive stroke and died. On November 7, 1888, he was laid to rest in the cemetery he had located for young Peter Gibson 25 years earlier. A Welsh miner wrote: "I went over from Van Winkle to attend his funeral. There was a big crowd. But there would have been more had he been rich. It is that way."

The Cameron Company Claim. C. Fulton took this photo on August 20, 1863. The four men seated on the log from left to right are: Alexander, John and Roderick Cameron and R. Stevenson. Standing are: William Stewart, A.D. McInnes, Jim Cummings, James Steele, James Wattie, William Schuyler, Robert Flynn at the corner post and George Black with the shovel and wheel barrow. This is one of the few Barkerville photos where men are identified.

The Diller Company

Finding gold was not a matter of luck. Letters, journals and mining documents show time and again that gold was found by men who had three attributes—experience, capital and determination. The story of Isaiah P. Diller and Company is an example.

Diller was a farmer's son in Pennsylvania when he heard of gold along the Fraser River. He borrowed money from his widowed mother and was among the first to test the bars of the Fraser River. By November 1858 Diller was in Yale, chairman of a miner's meeting asking for removal of the corrupt Commissioner of Crown Lands Richard Hicks.

In June 1860 he sold his rights in the White Mill claim, "consisting of 75 feet of ground to Ah Sun (Chinaman) for the sum of $25. Also one small cabin." Diller was on his way north.

Diller "threw in" with W.R. "Doc" Keithley and Henry Wolf. They staked a claim on the North Fork of the Quesnel River, near Quesnelle Forks, in October 1860. But they kept moving and staked another claim near Wolf Gulch, above Keithley Creek. This proved a rich find which provoked a minor rush and subsequently the town of Keithley Creek. Diller now had experience and capital.

Diller moved north again and by October 1861 he and James Loring of Boston had two claims near Richfield. They were then joined by Hardy Curry, a Georgia boy known as Hard Curry. The three moved down the creek and staked a claim on the right bank across from Stouts Gulch in September 1861. It was known as the Hard Curry or Diller claim. This is where the determination came in.

For 17 months they dug with no results. Despite sinking two shafts, moving tons of rock and gravel and employing 21 men and investing close to $8000 (about $200,000 in today's terms) they had no encouraging results.

On February 18, 1863, they began their washup and in three days brought in 25 pounds of gold worth $4720. The old gold-bearing creek channel they had been digging for was struck; they had hit the lead. During the next eight weeks they produced 10,653 ounces at a value of $170,448. The net profit was $135,976, $43,325 per share, close to $1 million each in today's money.

Diller, all 240 pounds of him, had said he wouldn't leave until he had his weight in gold. He left with his weight and his 120-pound dog's weight in gold.

In July, as production lagged, the partners hired an armed escort and headed south. According to the *British Columbian* newspaper, Diller had already brought down $130,000 in April. The claim continued to produce but not to the extent it did the first season. The three partners suffered a varied fate.

As the Diller story goes, he arrived at his Pennsylvania home just as the family farm was being auctioned off to pay taxes and a mortgage. Diller, unrecognized after so many years' absence, was the high bidder, then revealed himself to his aging mother and gave her the deed. He later moved to Oregon, where he married for the second time and then to Seattle with a third wife. Family records indicate he owned or built the Diller Hotel, the first Seattle hotel with an elevator.

Hard Curry lost his fortune in unsuccessful mining ventures and died in California in the 1870s. James D. Loring opened a Williams Creek Saloon with Hurdy Gurdy girls and brought one of the first pianos into Cariboo. He died April 29, 1874, of lung fever.

The Overlanders crossed the prairies of central Canada using the time-tested Red River carts. These were abandoned at Fort Edmonton. W.G. Hind sketch. PAC #28245

The Overlanders

"Gold in the Cariboo." The headlines of a new Cariboo gold strike on Williams Creek in 1861 attracted would-be miners and fortune hunters from the mines of California, the rough coast of Scotland, the slums of London and the farms of British Loyalists in Canada West.

In eastern Canada, men banded together in home-town groups to begin what was purported to be an easy five-week journey across the prairies and through the Rocky Mountains. This route was chosen in part because it was much cheaper than the long, uncomfortable ocean voyage by Panama and there was the feeling that establishment of a western route through "All British Territory" would stop U.S. expansionist moves.

From Canada the Overlanders traveled by rail and steamer to Wisconsin, then by Mississippi riverboat to St. Paul, Minnesota, on the edge of the frontier. By stagecoach, foot and sternwheeler they travelled north through a country about to erupt in a bloody war with the Sioux. As the sternwheeler *International* pulled into the Fort Garry dock on her maiden voyage, the people of Red River Settlement (now Winnipeg, Manitoba) gave a hearty cheer for "The Overlanders." Thus began a trek destined to become a legend.

Only at Fort Garry did the 250 Overlanders realize the extent of the vast and harsh country they were about to enter and how ill-equipped and inexperienced they were. Men who had never spent a night under canvas, ridden a horse, harnessed an ox, walked more than a couple of miles, been hungry or even cooked their own meals or washed their own clothes were about to embark on a journey across half a continent. The journey would take four months; seven men would die.

At Fort Garry the many small home-town groups formed into three major parties, based on religion, temperance, friendship, nationality and, finally, leadership and route. Fortunately, there were men among the 250 with the experience and leadership qualities to pull them together. The main party under Thomas McMicking left Fort Garry on June 2, 1862.

The route they took is paralleled today by the Yellowhead Highway. Week after week, month after month the Overlanders trudged westward: across the hot, flat, plains, through rivers, over hills, through muskeg, then over the mountains to Tête Jaune Cache on the Fraser River headwaters. By this time they were short of provisions. Some of the men were showing symptoms of scurvy; all were hungry. The Overlanders divided into two parties—one going south by way of Albreda Pass and the Thompson River to Fort Kamloops, the other larger party building rafts and dugout canoes to float the Fraser to Quesnellemouth and, with luck, the goldfields of Cariboo.

By the time they reached Quesnellemouth, autumn leaves were dropping and miners were heading south for the winter. A few Overlanders persisted and went on to Barkerville, but most wintered on the coast and returned the following spring. Eighty-nine Overlanders spent at least one season on Williams Creek. Many stayed in British Columbia and several stayed in Barkerville, operating businesses, mines and ranches and becoming important provincial pioneers.

The Rennie Story

On the walls of the Masonic Temple hangs an 1869 photograph of members of Cariboo Lodge #469, bedecked in lodge finery, standing on a rugged, half-cleared hillside. On the extreme right a man faces the camera with a hard countenance, a look of bitterness, perhaps of anger. His name is William Rennie, and his expression reflects a story of terror and tragedy.

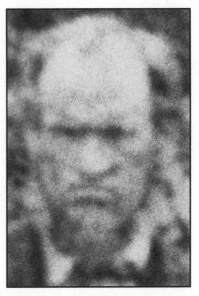

William Rennie, Overlander

Long after the main group of Overlanders reached Quesnellemouth and dispersed to their winter retreats, five men still trekked westward, victims of procrastination. Leaving their eastern home late in the season, they reached the Rockies with good traveling weather long past. The group comprised the three Rennie brothers—William, Gilbert and Thomas—John Helstone and John R. Wright, all natives of London, Canada West. They left London May 15, 1862, reached Fort Garry July 7 and Fort Edmonton the end of August. Returning Métis guides passed the news that the vanguard Overlanders had reached the Fraser River headwaters with few problems, other than a shortage of provisions.

The temptation was to stay at Fort Edmonton, as some other Overlanders had, to work the North Saskatchewan River for gold. The Rennie party was warned—an autumn crossing was dangerous. But weighing heavily on the other side was their desire to reach Cariboo. As winter closed in they pushed west. On October 4, 1862, they reached Tête Jaune Cache on the Fraser. The headwaters camp was trampled, littered and cleared by the 200 men who had passed a few weeks before. It was with difficulty that the five located two cotton-woods large enough to make dugout canoes. While a couple worked with axes, adzes and fire to hollow the canoes, the others killed the four oxen, their walking larder, and jerked the meat. Eleven days passed. On October 17, as the cold winds whistled winter up the Fraser River, they lashed their two canoes together and pushed into the current.

The water was low, fast, and the five men paddled quickly, not stopping to prospect the numerous bars and creeks along the way. Then on October 29, in the Giscome Rapids, several miles of rock-studded river two days out of Fort George, disaster struck. The two canoes wrapped broadside around a half-submerged rock. No matter what maneuver they tried, the canoe remained firmly stuck. Hours passed and the sun sank, drawing the cold curtain of night around five men huddled in the middle of the river.

For three freezing days the men were stranded until William Rennie carved thongs from a moosehide and braided a rope with which one man swam and pulled the others to shore. The men's frostbitten fingers could not light a fire, so they spent another night huddling together. On the fourth day John Helstone and Thomas Rennie woke with frozen feet. In desperation they managed to light a fire with gunpowder, and their hopes soared with the flames.

On the sixth day they attempted to reload the canoes and continue. When this failed, they decided that Gilbert and William Rennie would walk to Fort George for help. On November 4, one week after striking the rock, the two men set off, anticipating a journey of a couple days. A storm blew in, snow fell, ever deeper, ever more difficult to push through. A river crossing took three days, and still there was no sight of the fort. They shot a mink, a squirrel, a few grouse and ate handsful of rose hips. Williams Rennie's feet became frostbitten; his pace slowed to a shuffle. The days grew into an agonizing blur. The journey through winter to the safety of Fort George did not take two days or two weeks. It took 28 days.

At Fort George, Hudson's Bay Company Factor Thomas Charles told them he could not send help. The trail was impassable and the river not solid enough for travel. Without a rescue party, a slow, cold, certain death awaited the Rennies' brother Thomas, John Helstone and John Wright. Gilbert and William assuaged their consciences with the belief that, given their own difficulties, the other three could not have survived. But 90 miles upstream the men were living a winter hell.

The three men in the river camp had 10 days' food and plenty of firewood, so there had been no immediate sense of dread. Soon, they thought, a rescue party would arrive. Then the storm came. Their frostbitten limbs screamed in agony and rendered them unable even to search for firewood. By the time Gilbert and William Rennie reached Fort George, the three stranded men were in terrible pain and dreadful condition, but they were alive. They waited, and as they waited the fire burned out. They could not relight it.

Fort George Factor Charles pressured the two Rennie brothers to move on. Provisions were short. So on January 26, 1863, they headed south for Quesnellemouth.

Incredibly, after two months, two of the three men upriver still clung to life, still waited for rescue. When a wandering band of Carrier Indians stumbled on their camp they found two men eating the flesh of the third. The survivors drove the Indians away at gunpoint. Two weeks later the Indians returned to the river camp, this time to kill the devils who ate human flesh. As the sole survivor struggled on rotting limbs to escape, he was killed by repeated hatchet blows.

Months later the whole story unfolded when black trapper John Giscome found the camp. His Indian companions, frightened of "whiteman's justice," showed him where all the belongings were. Giscome buried the grisly remains of the tragedy.

The two surviving Rennies worked the winter near Williams Lake and then travelled to Williams Creek. Gilbert suffered from rheumatism so they left on June 17, 1863. Not for some months yet would the Giscome story reach the two men. Gilbert soon returned east to his wife and family. William was back in Barkerville by June 6, 1867, where he advertised in the *Cariboo Sentinel* as a boot and shoemaker.

The Masons of Barkerville, Cariboo Lodge No. 469. William Rennie is sitting on the right of the middle row. UBC

In the Great Fire of 1868 Rennie lost his shop and goods, valued at $1000, but opened again on September 22, 1868. Rennie stayed in Barkerville running his store and investing in claims such as the Murtle Company and the Proserpine Gold and Silver Company until about 1879. August 29, 1880, the Reverend Sexsmith married William Rennie and Mrs. Catherine Evans at the home of lumber merchant I.B. Nason. Catherine was the widow of Captain John Evans, of Welsh Adventurers fame, who died at Stanley almost exactly a year before.

The rest of their lives, and their deaths, passed unnoticed and unrecorded. Of William Rennie all that remains is a likeness in a Masonic Lodge photograph.

John Bowron, Overlander

John Bowron, the son of William Bowron and Sarah Odell, was born in Huntingdon, Quebec, March 10, 1837. William Bowron was a Yorkshireman who emigrated to New York and set up a business in lumber and general merchandise. During the War of 1812 he moved to Huntingdon, Quebec, and married Sarah, daughter of Colonel Odell of Odellstown, Quebec. Their son, John Bowron, was a tall, slim, young man of 25 studying law when news of the British Columbia goldfields reached him.

He took only a moment to pack up and join the Huntingdon party of Overlanders heading west. The party of over 25 men became an integral part of Barkerville's life. It included men like the Wattie and Sellars brothers, *Cariboo Sentinel* founder George Wallace, Peter McIntyre, William Gage, blacksmith William B. Cameron, George Tunstall and William B. Schuyler, the latter two being schoolmates of John Bowron.

John Bowron at age 32.
PABC #49409

Bowron wintered at Victoria and then, in the early spring, he and partner Bill Schuyler trekked north to the gold creeks, where they were issued mining licences, #256 for Bowron and #255 for Schuyler, on May 11, 1863. John Bowron did whatever work he could—carpentry, cleaning out sluice boxes, separating gold from sand, and digging in a shaft—until he found an opening in the government service.

While maintaining an interest in certain gold claims, Bowron took on an increasing number of responsibilities; in 1864 he became librarian; in 1866, postmaster; in 1872, mining recorder and constable at Richfield; in 1875, government agent; in 1883, gold commissioner.

Bowron firmly believed that the true wealth of Barkerville would be found in the "mother lode" or gold quartz veins, and although he was scoffed at, he persisted and eventually convinced the government to put some effort into exploration. When Bowron's belief in the gold quartz veins proved justified, there was a flurry of excitement. But costs were too high and capital investment money was short, so no attempt was made to retrieve the gold until the opening of the Cariboo Gold Quartz Mine in the 1930s.

In 1869 John Bowron married Emily Penberthy Edwards, an American woman 13 years his junior. They had five children—John, William, Alice, Lottie and Archie. William built the house across the street from the family home and then moved away, as did all the others, although Lottie frequently returned. Both John and Emily were active in the Cariboo Amateur Dramatic Association and were considered the elite of Barkerville. John Bowron rode through several changes of government and as a courteous, kindly, generous man was a most respected citizen and government official.

The Bowron social position was fostered and enjoyed by Emily and capricious daughter Lottie, who for many years was an important member of the self-appointed Barkerville upper crust. Lottie married Dr. George Tunstall in December 1889. He was the son of George Tunstall, Overlander, a boyhood friend of John Bowron. Dr. Tunstall had an office in the "Dr. Hugh Watt" building and was a surgeon at the hospital. The marriage appears short-lived for Lottie was soon using her maiden name again. Dr. Tunstall returned to his family home in Kamloops in 1902.

Barkerville was a mature mining town when the Bowrons lived here. The population was stable, although the economy was still based on gold, and miners and prospectors still came and went. Lottie's schoolmates included Nettie House and Johnny Houser, long-time residents. In Lottie's later years, she had vivid memories of the town and its life:

I used to waken in the morning to the sound of rushing Williams Creek and the song of the anvil from the O'Neil blacksmith's shop across the street and the sound of Billy Hodgkinson's pack horse with a bell carrying milk up town from the milk ranch down the road.

Another cheery sound was the water dripping into the water barrel in the wood shed. This had to be brought from the springs on the hillside in overhead wooden troughs, and to the backs of the various homes by smaller troughs. Can't you hear the arguments and tempers rising on wash day when the first house took more than its share of the precious water?

On the cold cold days the sound of the frost and snow crackled beneath our feet on the sidewalks as we ran home from school for our

Bowron with daughters Allie and Lottie circa 1900. PABC #68823

lunches. On those bitter days mother usually had a big pot of hot pea soup on the stove in the front room. Most of the house had to be closed off to keep us warm.

I recall the anxiety lest the snow should not have gone by May 24th so that we girls might wear our summer dresses for the usual picnic at Joe Mason's meadows up at Jack O' Clubs Lake.

And then the lovely walks with Mother up to Richfield, through Chinatown, past Stout's Gulch and the canyon, where Billy Barker sank his shaft. The walk was to bring my father home. His office was in the old courthouse...

Then the dogs—such a part of us—with the surnames of the family they belonged to always attached to them, such as Jack Kelly, Jeff Mason, Crib House, Tinker Bowron, etc.

The exciting arrival of the stage on Thursday evening and its departure Saturday morning—everyone was excited when the stage came in—the children watched for it behind the church—then the cry being carried from one child to another—"Here, here's the stage, here's the stage."

If you've never travelled by the "BX" Barnard's Express then you've never travelled. Four days from here to Ashcroft—the lovely spirited horses, the heavy red coaches. And to get to sit next to the driver on the box—that was almost heaven.

If to others in the outside world we seemed to live in a queer place we as children knew nothing of this, and to us our lives were quite natural and complete.

Emily Bowron died in Barkerville in 1895, and in 1897 John Bowron, then 60, married 33-year-old Elizabeth Watson at Victoria. The couple had one child, Aileen Genevieve Leone. John Bowron died in Victoria on September 6, 1906, just as he retired. His second wife Elizabeth died in 1922, and his daughter Lottie in 1964. John Bowron's name is remembered in Bowron Lake Provincial Park, a few miles east of Barkerville.

The Company of Welsh Adventurers

Cariboo gold attracted many interesting men, and Captain John Evans of Machynlleth in North Wales was certainly one. Evans was employed at a cotton factory and had invested in quarries and became inspired to organize a Cariboo expedition of 24 Welsh Adventurers. While Evans took a short-cut via the Panama to scout their prospects, the other men traveled to Victoria via Cape Horn.

While awaiting their arrival on the *Rising Sun,* he went up the Fraser to Quesnellemouth then arranged with Governor Douglas for the lease of a large mining claim on Lightning Creek. The lease was unusual, for by regulation miners had to work their own claims or a combination of claims. Evans used the threat of all British capital being withdrawn if allowances were not made.

Evans' men arrived in Victoria in June 1863 after a six-month sea voyage, and proceeded to their crown-lease creek, a laborious five-week journey. The Adventurers mined here for two seasons with expenses of over $26,000 and retrieved only $450 in gold. For some time men had been deserting, and when the venture finally failed in the fall of 1864 all but Evans and a few others scattered.

Captain John Evans was a pious puritan who once said that he would like to find just one good mine so that he might give all the proceeds to the Booth Street Welsh Congregational Chapel in Manchester, which he had helped found. He came from a country with sharp religious divisions and was surprised to find that colonial divisions were blurred, and the community lacked his morality. Evans

The Aurora Claim, June 15, 1867. The wash-up that day was 485 ounces.
PABC #22924

deplored the fact that on Sunday, the Lord's Day, gambling, swearing and other vices continued at an uproarious level. To counter this immorality, Evans and a few of his men built a small hall in Barkerville on a lot granted by Gold Commissioner Cox. It was called the Cambrian Hall and served as a meeting hall and a place for religious services until it was burned in the Great Fire of 1868.

Many coveted the valuable property near the Methodist church. With the hall's destruction, there was a rush for the land. When unauthorized building began, Evans appealed to Magistrate Chartres Brew in March 1869, stating the offer from Cox and explaining, "Some have gone so far as to commence building in such a manner as to completely block up the entrance to the Hall, thereby rendering it nothing less than back premises to a saloon and something worse.

"The building [the old Cambrian Hall] was the only Protestant place open for religious purposes throughout Cariboo during a period of two to three years, it was also entirely unsectarian."

The land title was granted, the claim jumpers evicted and a new Cambrian Hall was built.

In 1875 Evans was elected to the Legislative Assembly of British Columbia, and in 1877 he was married (for the third time) to Catherine Jones, a woman who brought him great happiness. Unfortunately, the happiness was short-lived. In June 1879 he wrote to his children that his rheumatism was bothering him. On August 25, 1879, he suffered inflammation of the bowels and kidneys and died at Stanley. His friends wrote on his grave marker, "Blessed are the dead who died in the Lord..."

The Cattle Drovers

Fresh beef, pork and mutton were so important tc carnivorous miners that they were willing to pay the outrageous price of fifty cents a pound. Men with a ranching background found selling cattle a quicker way to prosperity than digging in cold gravel.

Six such men were the Van Volkenburgh brothers, Benjamin, Abraham and Isaac; the two Harpers, Jerome and Thaddeus, and Edward Toomey. Toomey was a butcher with a Barkerville store and abattoir. The Harpers were experienced cattle drovers with grasslands in the interior already preempted by the early 1860s. The Van Volkenburghs, Americans of Dutch extraction, added manpower to run several stores in various gold camps.

Cattle drives often came directly up the main street of Barkerville, providing an exciting event for the town's children.

The Harpers were from Tucker Co. West Virginia. Jerome, born in 1826, left Tucker Co. with three brothers in the late 1840s to try their luck in California. Seeing yet another opportunity they sent Jerome to open a store in Chili, South America. He was doing a good business when a rebellion erupted. Jerome, a confederate supporter, backed the rebels and was banished to Patagonia, where he was rescued by his brother Capt. Harper.

Jerome and Thaddeus, then aged 23 and 22, were farming in Santa Clara Co. California in 1852. In 1858 they came north, and by 1859 they operated a sawmill at Yale but spent enough time in Victoria to become part of a Confederate plan to outfit a ship. The plan failed and the Harpers settled in to business, bidding on a road contract and gathering land.

As the Cariboo rush created a demand for supplies, they started driving in cattle from Washington and Oregon. Dr. Cheadle, in his 1863 *Journal of a Trip Across Canada,* says "Jerome Harper arrived on Horseback; he was bringing in a drove of 500 cattle from Oregon; a Virginian and staunch supporter of the South he said he was bitter because his mother and family had been driven out of their homes in Virginia where they had nice estates and left penniless."

Soon the brothers had ranches at Cache Creek, Harper's Camp near Kamloops and in the Chilcotin country. They started another sawmill at Quesnellemouth, a flour mill near Clinton, and a partnership with Tormey and Van Volkenburghs.

Jerome was the businessman. Things began to fail in the early 1870s when Jerome was kicked in the face by a horse, suffering a broken skull. He retired to California, where he was described as being insane, and drowned in his bathtub in Santa Barbara November 27, 1874. Thaddeus fought with the family, gained the land and businesses and carried on. He started a cattle drive to Chicago but diverted to California. In the 1880s he organized the present-day Gang Ranch and gradually increased the acreage to over one million. Thaddeus also became active in mining again, with claims near Stanley and on the Horsefly River. That area also became known as Harper's Camp but was changed to Horsefly in 1921.

By 1890 Thaddeus had sold out his mine leases and the ranches, but the JH brand, one of the first to sear a hide in B.C., is still being heated in branding fires today. Thaddeus retired to Victoria where he died in 1898.

To satisfy the need for fresh meat during Cariboo rush, the Harpers, Toomey and the Van Volkenburghs formed a company, Messrs. Van Volkenburgh & Co., with shops in Richfield, Barkerville, Cameronton and other camps advertising "a large supply of the best Meat always on hand." The partnership virtually monopolized the cattle industry for over a decade, and in various forms started the largest ranches in the province.

In 1868 a writer noted, "We paid a visit this week to the abattoir of Messrs. Van Volkenburgh and Co., with their extensive contiguous warehouse, built and fitted up expressly for storing fresh meat for winter use. Messrs. Van Volkenburgh & Co. have been killing off stock for winter for the last few weeks, the last lot of which, consisting of over 30 head, were just brought in by Messrs. Harper & Toomey."

In December 1869 the *Cariboo Sentinel* noted, "Van Volkenburgh

& Co., the enterprising butchers, have slaughtered 360 sheep, and stored them in a clean and airy place, in the storehouse just above the gorge. Messrs. V. intend to bring more to the knife, so that we shall have a plentiful supply of fresh though frozen, mutton during the

The pack train of Red Headed Davis crossing the Quesnel River. These pack trains brought in all the supplies for the gold fields until the road was completed in 1865. VCA #P909

winter." The firm's slaughter houses and those of Gannon and Company were in the large clearing seen today on the cemetery road.

These slaughter houses depended on other drovers' bringing in cattle as well. A typical herd would be 400 head of steers, 50 milk cows and 50 horses. While the Harpers managed to corner the market, there were many other drovers. General Joel Palmer was the first. He brought a cattle herd and several wagons of merchandise north in 1858 and again in 1859.

The Jeffrey brothers of Alabama came through in 1859 or 60 with cattle, and in 1861 Major Thorpe of Yakima, Washington, Ben E. Snipes, William Gates and William Murphy all brought herds north. Lewis Campbell joined John Wilson to bring in 300 head and later settled near Kamloops. Wilson had already been to the goldfields and was gathering land at Grand Prairie, where he would become the cattle King of the Thompson country.

Daniel Drumheller brought a herd west from what later became Alberta, and Aschal Sumner Bates bought cattle for his spreads on the Thompson and near 150 Mile House. By the height of the Cariboo rush in 1862, drovers were bring in over 4000 cattle per year, a total of over 21,000 by 1868, when the province began to gain self-sufficiency in the beef market.

As well as the cattle trailed in from the south, the Williams Creek area was the site of at least four "milk ranches." These were situated along the meadows toward Wells and in the Pleasant Valley area. In 1867 the *Cariboo Sentinel* said they totaled 80 cows, producing enough milk for the whole of Williams Creek and Lowhee Gulch, at "the moderate price of $1 per gallon."

Ranchers and farmers were attracted by the fortunes of the gold fields, but many of them stayed and settled the rich grasslands of the province, starting a thriving industry that continues today.

This woman on the balcony of the Hotel de France illustrates the separateness of women on the creeks. It is likely the woman is Julia Picot, who bought the hotel in 1869. PABC #5169

The Women of Williams Creek

A Newfoundland riddle asks: "Who was born, lived, but had no name?" The answer is Lot's wife. It would be equally correct to answer, "The Women of Williams Creek." They were born, lived on the creeks, had children, ran businesses, but with few exceptions their names remain unknown. The newspaper items, the pioneer profiles, the obituaries, all are male dominated. The best examples are the birth announcements. Example: *Cariboo Sentinel*, June 18, 1866, "Birth, at Barkerville, 15 inst., wife of William A. Meacham, a son." Or November 27, 1869: "Mr. Fick, the proprietor of the New England Bakery, has returned...with his wife."

Hurdy dancers and prostitutes were usually referred to by their first name, or a nickname, if at all. Madams and business women were known by their last name, when mentioned. But it is possible by compiling enough records to come up with a faint portrait of women on the creeks.

Despite beliefs to the contrary, the creeks were not devoid of women. There may not have been many, but they were here, and as individuals had a greater effect on the social structure and business than any single man, the Camerons and Barkers aside.

In the decade beginning 1862, over 150 women can be accounted for by name. Women were close behind the first men who reached the creeks. Harry Guillod found miners' wives and children on Lightning Creek in 1862. Nine prostitutes paraded Williams Creek that summer, and women opened saloons, whiskey shops, boarding houses and restaurants. When winter came they headed south. Mrs. Mary Ann Webster and her two daughters, one of whom was Margaret Cusheon, a saloon keeper's wife, were lost in a snow storm on Bald Mountain for several days. Johanna Maguire, a prostitute heading south, was lost for a week and reported dead. She found herself, but lost the $3000 she had made that season in her own gold rush.

The first winter following Barker's strike, only 90 people stayed on Williams Creek; seven were women. They deserve recognition: Rosa Donnelly, wife of a miner; Anna Cameron, wife of hotel keeper Richard Cameron, and her sister Lizzie Roddy, who later married A.D. McInnes; Sophia Cameron, wife of John A. "Cariboo" Cameron, who died that winter of typhoid; Scotch Jenny, Mrs. Janet Morris, a merchant's wife; Mary Winnard, wife of blacksmith William Winnard and an unnamed French woman.

The following season a steady influx of women began. Eliza Barker came her with her new husband Billy; Eliza Bailley opened a whiskey shop; Lizzie Boardman, Louisa Cunningham, Jessie Heatherington came with their miner husbands; the Brown family opened a hotel in Richfield; Mrs. Nathan, aka Mary Boyle, opened a brothel, as did Mary Sheldon, Fanny Bendixon and likely Julia Picot; Mrs. F. W. Dustin opened a boarding house on Conklin Gulch; Rebecca Gibbs, a black woman, began a laundry; Florence Wilson, Mme. Lamon, Mme. Lawrent, all opened saloons.

Many of these women were active socially. Florence Wilson started a public library, and Jennie Allen, Johanna Maguire and others were known for nursing sick and injured miners. Catherine Parker and her daughter and Florence Wilson were also active in the Cariboo Amateur Dramatic Society, and Mrs. Tracey sang at church.

Women also applied for mining certificates, though whether they mined or took an active part in the claim is debatable. Certainly Margaret Cusheon and Eliza Ord appear to have been active in claim affairs, but most women's licences were likely just a way for their husbands to hold an extra share, or work another claim in their name.

Many, if not most, women who came to the creeks married here. Often this documentation tells of a past life. Obituaries are edited for refinement and respectability. A former dance hall girl is remembered posthumously as a midwife; a prostitute's past is forgotten.

Many of these gold rush women bore children here. Anna Cameron was the first; October 25, 1862, at the Pioneer Hotel in

Cameronton, Allan Richfield Cameron was born. Miners lined up to have his aunt Anne Roddie allow them to hold the child. It was a rough land, with primitive medical facilities. Wellington Moses made frequent notes in his diary about women like Mrs. Frances Lee or Mrs. Fred Rose losing a child or the stillborn child of Eleanor Edwards.

When their men died, as men in the goldfields frequently did, no woman remained a widow long, except by choice. Shortly following the required year's mourning, they were remarried. Catherine Parker became Mrs. Austin; Catherine Evans married William Rennie when Capt. Evans died; Ellen Peebles remarried, to William Wormald; Scotch Jenny Morris became Janet Allen. Subsequent census records show the blended families of Cariboo.

Divorces appear to be uncommon but are also poorly recorded. Anna Cameron divorced Richard and married Benjamin Van Volkenburgh, and Margaret Waddell went to court to have Florence Wilson pay a bill, pleading her position as a divorced woman. Often these women were referred to politely as widows, or grass widows.

Williams Creek women died of old age, heart attacks and, like Mary Wintrip, of suicide at the end of a depression.

The Demimonde—women of the town

Not all the women on the creek were kindly and respectable. Jane Snyder got Joseph Shearer drunk and had him sign over all his claims to her. The court had little sympathy and awarded each of them half. Madam J.B.A. Reviere, likely a prostitute, fell in lust with Cariboo sheriff Daniel Chisholm. They fled Williams Creek, abandoned her child in Victoria and escaped to California. Chisholm was married, with children in the east. Another unknown woman abandoned her newborn or stillborn child to the waters of Williams Creek.

And there is no doubt that Williams Creek had plenty of brothels and individual prostitutes, for where there were men and money prostitution was sure to flourish.

The role of madams, prostitutes and brothels in Barkerville is poorly documented—not surprising, given Victorian morality—but a few references appeared in newspapers. One such reference appeared in the *Colonist* of September 10, 1862, and was copied later in the San Francisco papers, reinforcing an image of Barkerville as a coarse, rough, mining town.

"THE PROSTITUTES: on the creek—nine in number—put on great airs. They dress in male attire and swagger through the saloons and mining camps with cigars or huge qwids of tobacco in their mouths, cursing and swearing and look like anything but the angels in petticoats heaven intended they should be. Each has a revolver or bowie knife attached to her waist, and it is quite a common occurrence to see one or more women dressed in male attire playing poker in the saloons, or drinking whiskey at the bars. They are a degraded set, and all good men in the vicinity wish them hundreds of miles away."

These women were likely those who were categorized as the street-level prostitute. They were followed by the madams who ran the parlour houses, the saloons with extra rooms for sexual dalliances. The line between respectability and a disorderly house is blurred by time.

Prostitutes' success relied on keeping a low profile, so they remain hidden, except where they were dragged into the public eye. Hattie Lucas was one such. She threw stones at the house of Mary Sheldon, a madam. Lucas was described as, "a tall and graceful young woman, having considerable personal attractions, but unfortunately a passion so uncontrollable that even the gravity of the court could not restrain its outbursts."

Then William Williams, a miner who made a habit of assaulting women, pulled her off her horse and knocked her down three times. Williams got three months. He later assaulted Elizabeth Thurber, a hotel and saloon keeper.

Sheldon, alias Slap-Jack Johnny, had a tough time with the law in Victoria so headed to Barkerville where she opened a brothel. She was described as "a buxom middle-aged woman of matronly appearance, whom the Court characterized as being of sober steady habits." Obviously the court was willing to overlook a few indiscretions. Sheldon often travelled to Yale with other single women and may have been running a brothel circuit, common in California.

Mary Nathan was married to Samuel in Australia, had a child, moved to California, and set up shop in Victoria where she was known as a Judy, a prostitute, and Samuel as a keeper of a disorderly house, a brothel. They had a falling out, and Mary divorced him, sort of, and came to Barkerville and was involved with several men who helped her get started in a saloon. She died in Barkerville in 1878.

Eliza Ord came to view when she went on a rampage and broke all the windows in the home of James Bruce. She had come to Barkerville as a miner's wife and kept a variety of establishments after leaving him. She was in and out of court, often as plaintiff. She sued Robert Drinkall for breach of a marriage contract, but it was thrown out of court. Eventually she retired to California but came back ten years later to reclaim a share in a claim. She charged a judge with pocketing the money, was committed to the insane asylum but released by New Westminster doctors who claimed she was quite sane. Back in Barkerville she laid counter charges against constable Lindsay and drifted into history.

This was not an easy life, and law was on the side of men. Assault was not uncommon. As a case study, consider Sophia Rouillard, one of several French women in town. She came to town at age 25, likely only for a summer. A miner owed her money. When she asked for payment he punched her hard in the stomach. She remarked, "that blow will be the death of me." Two weeks later she died.

Dr. Bell was called in to examine her for the coroner. He said she drank too much. He forgot she had complained of her stomach's being on fire. Witnesses saw the blow being struck, testified to her illness, knew the miner. The all-male jury agreed with the doctor: Sophia had died from a visitation of God, brought on by strong drink. It was a case that was repeated over and over. And their graves are unmarked, unrecorded.

Hurdy Gurdy Girls

The Hurdy Gurdy Girls were dancing girls, "terpsichorean artistes," brought from Germany, "direct from Baden Baden," usually via California, by an entrepreneurial saloon keeper. While Barry and Adler of the Fashion Saloon are credited with being the first, it is at best a doubtful claim. Also doubtful is the suggestion that French madam Fanny Bendixon was in charge of them. No contemporary documentation links her with the dancers.

Four sober Hurdies pose on the town boardwalk in uniforms of red dress and waist-slimming belt. PABC #95344

In fact, James Loring, of the Diller claim fame, may have been the first to bring in dancing partners for miners. In 1865, perhaps sooner, he was employing native women at his Terpsychorean [sic] Saloon in Cameronton. From that time on native women were a part of the underside of Barkerville's social life, most often surfacing as prostitutes such as Lucy Bones or Gentle Annie.

It appears the hurdies first arrived on the creek in the summer of 1866, dancing in their celebrated style at the Fashion Saloon and Martin's Saloon. By the next summer they were also enticing miners into Jacob Mundorf's Crystal Palace Saloon and soon to Sterling's saloon. Their name came from the hand organs that were used to accompany their dancing, but in Barkerville the accompanying instrument seems to have been the fiddle. "Hurdies" is also an old English term for the buttocks or the hips.

One dance cost a miner $1. The girls then got a percentage of any drinks they enticed miners to buy. And entice they did, for some miners were reported to be broke, having spent all their earnings on the hurdies. They were not prostitutes, according to the *Cariboo Sentinal*. But judging by hurdy houses in California, prostitution was certainly part of the business. In 1866 the *Sentinel* ran a letter describing the Hurdies.

HURDY GURDY DAMSELS. There are three descriptions of the above named "Ladies" here, they are unsophisticated maidens of Dutch extraction, from "poor but honest parents" and morally speaking, they really are not what they are generally put down for. They are generally brought to America by some speculating, conscienceless scoundrel of a being commonly called a "Boss Hurdy". This man binds them in his service until he has received about a thousand per cent for his outlay. The girls receive a few lessons in the terpsichorean art, are put into a kind of uniform, generally consisting of a red waist, cotton print skirt and a half mourning headdress resembling somewhat in shape the top knot of a male turkey, this uniform gives them quite a grotesque appearance. Few of them speak English, but they soon pick up a few popular vulgarisms; if you bid one of them good morning your answer will likely be "itsh sphlaid out" or "you bet your life."

The Hurdy style of dancing differs from all other schools. If you ever saw a ring of bells in motions, you have seen the exact positions these young ladies are put through during their dance, the more muscular the partner, the nearer the approximation of the ladies' pedal extremities to the ceiling, and the gent who can hoist his "gal" the highest is considered the best dancer; the poor girls as a general thing earn their money very hardly.

James Anderson, Bard of Cariboo, wrote a song about the Hurdies. It was sung to the tune of "Green Grow the Rushes Oh!" Anderson's song was published in the *Cariboo Sentinel,* July 23, 1866.

> *Last simmer we had lassies here*
> *Frae Germany—the Hurdies, O!*
> *And troth I wot, as I'm a Scot*
> *They were the bonnie hurdies, O!*
>
> *Chorus: Bonnie are the hurdies, O!*
> *The German hurdy-gurdies, O!*
> *The daftest hour that e'er I spent*
> *Was dancin' wi' the hurdies, O!*
>
> *They left the creek wi' lots o' gold,*
> *Danced frae orr lads sae clever, O!*
> *My blessin's on their "sour krout" heads.*
> *Gif they stay awa forever, O!*

Clearly James Anderson was not one of those who wept when the hurdies left for warmer climates in the fall. There may have been a language barrier and their morals may have been questioned by some, but not all hurdies left. Several stayed each fall to marry merchants and miners. Elizabeth Ebert married Edward Dougherty and moved to the Clinton area. Elizabeth Feiling married Samuel Walker, who kept a boarding house at Centreville on Mosquito Creek. Jeanette Ceise, a German girl who married John Houser in San Francisco, is thought to have been a hurdy and likewise the German wife of Italian merchant Angelo Pendolo. Jacob Mundorf fell under the charms of a dancer he hired, and married Katrina. Carpenter Joseph St. Laurent, later of Quesnel, married Georgina Wilhelmina Henrietta Nachtigall. And when the dance hall closed, Mrs. "Hurdy Billy" Hodgkinson, Isabella Irvine, married a miner and took in laundry.

Doubtless there were others. Martha O'Neill (later Boss) was raised in Barkerville and said, "Of course there were other 'Hurdy's' in the town too, all married and mostly with large families." Each of these women accepted the challenge of a new land and stayed to pioneer.

The last mention of the hurdies appears in 1871. By that time a hurdy named Rosa Haub was in change of the dancers and would go down to Victoria to bring new girls north. But Barkerville was fading and gold was scarce, so the "lady professors of the terpsichorean academy" drifted south to California. Rosa only got as far as Victoria, where she found an eligible bachelor.

Madam Fanny Bendixon

The enigmatic Fanny Bendixon came on the world's stage in San Francisco at about age 25, as the California gold rush waned. She was the mistress of a leading underworld figure, a beautiful and elegant woman dressed in furs, jewels and silks. Inexplicably, she became a virtuous woman overnight, began attending church every Sunday, shunned her former underworld companions and announced her marriage to Louis Bendixon. The change was not accomplished without difficulty, for her former suitor reacted violently. When gifts did not have the desired effect, he resorted to severe beatings and had acid thrown at her. Her resolve to reform intensified.

Fanny, and perhaps Louis, Bendixon, were likely part of the great migration from France following the Lottery of the Golden Ingots. This scheme of the French government dumped thousands of French criminals into California. Some wandered north.

Ingots found themselves unpopular in California, and perhaps that and a desire to start their own business prompted the Bendixons to move north to another coastal gold rush boomtown—Victoria. Here they built a modest two-storey brick hotel, the St. George's, which became known for its accommodating host and hostess. Gold rushes came and went, as did the prosperity they produced, and in a few years Victoria felt the effects of a recession. Business declined and the Bendixons' marriage collapsed. Louis returned to California, while Fanny held to her dream of opening a successful saloon. She saw that while Victoria was momentarily fading, there was money to be made in the high mountain creeks of Cariboo.

Fanny Bendixon was in Barkerville by June 1865, occupying a house on the main street next to Moses' barbershop. Somehow she borrowed or raised money and in June 1866 opened the first of several saloons. "Parlor Saloon, Barkerville. Madame Bendixon begs to announce to her friends that she has refitted this well known Saloon, where she invites the public to give her a call. The bar is stocked with the best of LIQUORS and SEGARS that can be procured." In California the term parlor saloon was understood to mean a saloon/brothel. By November 1866 the saloon was mentioned in the newspaper as being empty.

Fanny was not to be kept down. A year later she announced the opening of a second establishment: "Belle Union Saloon, kept by Mrs. Fanny Bendixon, Barkerville. This Saloon, which is fitted up in the most elegant style, has just been opened to the public. None but the best brands of LIQUORS and CIGARS served at the bar. This is a PRIVATE SALOON for the accommodation of customers."

Again, what a "PRIVATE SALOON" entailed in Barkerville is unclear, but to Californians it meant a doorman who only admitted those known to the establishment. The accommodation was taken care of by young women.

This saloon was lost in the fire of 1868 but rebuilt by contractors Bruce and Mann in November 1868.

The story takes a twist here. By most accounts Louis Bendixon retreated to California from Victoria, but a Louis Bendixon declared bankruptcy in B.C. on December 9, 1866, and appears as a saloon keeper in the Barkerville 1869 directory. Did Louis not go to California, or did he go and then return? And after this? Did Louis disappear again, or die and leave the saloon business to Fanny? In the 1881 census Fanny is a widow.

Also in 1869 there was a county court case involving Fanny Bendixon: James Burdick vs. Bruce and Mann. The court records indicate that contractors Bruce and Mann built a "house" for Burdick on a lot owned by Fanny Bendixon, "with whom Burdick is in partnership." Fanny held the liquor licence of this house, where the gross receipts of the bar were from $15 to $20 a day, rising to $25 and $50 a day around Christmas. "The house is also a hotel or boarding or rooming house—it has beds." There is a possibility that this "house with beds" was a brothel and that Burdick was the traditional male partner of a madam.

This establishment met with some success. Later Bendixon took advantage of the 1870s strikes in Van Winkle by opening the doors of the Van Winkle Saloon, then selling it in 1874 and opening the Exchange Saloon in Stanley, a stone's throw from Van Winkle. The Stanley saloon featured a reading room "with the latest periodicals and newspapers." The 1871 Barkerville Directory also connects Bendixon with the St. George Saloon, a name she brought from Victoria. Perhaps Fanny was in business with a number of Barkerville entrepreneurs who knew her success at saloon keeping.

By 1880 Fanny was back in Barkerville with a saloon and boarding house. In this last business, next to the Masonic lodge, she became a fixture of the town, the subject of reminiscences.

Charles O'Neil's daughter remembered her as a "fat and good-looking French woman; must have weighed some 300 averdupois [sic] and there she sat on two chairs amid her glasses and bottles, She had

Mrs. Janet Allen, known as Big Jennie and Scotch Jennie, ran the Pioneer Hotel at Mosquito Creek. The two men are Donald and James Rankin, successful miners. PABC #10154

nothing but smiles for the children (and often gave them 'British Sweeties') and called them 'cherie' but let an adult enter her shop and the air became blue with curses."

When Judge Matthew Begbie made a return visit to Cariboo in 1889 he wrote, "Madame Bendixon is here in great form, indeed enormous, vast, of undiscoverable girth, though she was always of goodly diameter."

Fanny maintained some contact with her family, for in 1897 she brought her grand niece Leonie Fanny to live with her, likely as a companion in her declining years. In Barkerville Leonie married Hugh Cochrane and they soon had a daughter, Clara Frances Leonie Douglas Cochrane, and in 1899 a son, Robert Hugh.

In January of 1899 Fanny was ill and realized it was time to make a will. In it she left Hugh Cochrane all her real estate in Barkerville and appointed him executor and trustee for the rest of her goods for the benefit of the Cochranes' daughter. Her niece, with whom she did not get along, she left nothing. She left her friend Frank Meyer $200 and gave her earrings to Elizabeth Kelly.

Leonie was not happy with the arrangement. She wanted the earrings, so she concocted a codicil to the will and had Fanny sign it in April, when she was barely coherent.

Fanny died on May 2, 1899, her age still a matter of conjecture. No sooner had she died than the court case began. Elizabeth Kelly wanted the earrings and sued. It was found that Leonie had not acted in good faith. Judge Clement Cornwall decided only Fanny's first will would be recognized, and awarded the earrings to Kelly.

Even in death Fanny Bendixon was a woman who captured the imagination of many and likely the hearts of many a miner and businessman along the creeks.

James Anderson - Bard of Cariboo

Every developing nation or region has its unofficial poet laureate. The Klondike had Robert Service; Australia, Banjo Paterson, and Cariboo had James Anderson, the Bard of Cariboo.

Anderson was born into a prominent family in Perthshire, Scotland, about 1838. He received a good education and was married in 1860. The following year he had a son. In 1863 Anderson left his family and like so many Scots before him crossed the ocean to seek his fortune in a new land.

The Prairie Flower Company. Most of the men in mining photographs are unidentified, as no one recorded their names. However, the man leaning against the post on the right is identified as poet James Anderson. UBC

Anderson's significance on Williams Creek is not because of any fortune he found as a partner in the Prairie Flower Co. and the Ayrshire Lass on Lightning Creek. He is remembered for the songs and poems he wrote, published and performed. Anderson became the miners' voice. The feelings he captured are preserved in the "Letters to Sawney" in Scotland from "his friend Jeams" in Cariboo. Anderson and a friend published a weekly manuscript that they read aloud in coffee saloons, and the *Cariboo Sentinel* often used his verse. He was an original member of the Cariboo Amateur Dramatic Association, where his writing and performing skills were in great demand. He often used tunes from popular songs and wrote words appropriate to the miners. In later years Anderson wrote that "barring Sawney's letters I would have been pleased had the others rhymes been buried in the tailings of Williams Creek. They were written on the spur of the moment, and for the moment and are not worthy of reproduction."

Yet decades later his rhymes such as "The Rough But Honest Miner," "Waiting for the Mail," "Dead Broke," "Hard Luck," "The Prospector's Shanty," "The Young Man from Canada," "The Dancing Girls of Cariboo," "The Bar Room Song," and many more were still remembered and repeated by Cariboo miners.

When Anderson left Cariboo in November 1871, he settled on one of his father's properties in Cupar, Fife, Scotland, and later moved to England, where he died in 1923. He did not take a fortune with him but left a fortune in words behind to be enjoyed by many generations. His last lines before leaving Cariboo are an appropriate epitaph.

> 'Twas all I asked of thee,
> One handful of thy plenteous golden grain,
> Had'st thou but yielded, I'd have sung "Farewell!"
>   And home again.

> But, time on time, defeat!
> Ah, cold and cruel, callous Cariboo!
> Have eight years' honest persevering toil
>   No more of you?

Once again James Anderson was speaking not only for himself but for those thousands of men and a few women who had asked for just one handful, and left defeated.

Judge Matthew Baillie Begbie

Matthew Baillie Begbie, often mislabeled the Hanging Judge, was a Scot, born in 1819 into a British Army family. When his father retired, the family settled in Guernsey off the coast of France. Young Begbie was a brilliant student, with skills in map making, mathematics and law. He was called to the bar in November 1844 and soon gained the attention of the Lord Chancellor in the Chancery Courts. This attention led to Begbie's appointment as Judge of British Columbia, the representative in all the courts of Her Majesty Queen Victoria. Begbie did not take his position lightly.

Judge Begbie's first circuit was in the spring of 1859 for the assizes—the trials of anyone accused of a crime. This first circuit established his reputation as a man who could debate, shoot, paddle,

Judge Matthew Baillie Begbie.
VPL #22860

fight, camp and eat with any official, miner or criminal that circumstance dictated. He stood over six feet tall, a powerful man in all respects. Though he was not a "hanging judge"—and sentenced only two Cariboo men to the scaffold—he was not one to treat crime lightly, and fear of his sentences deterred outlaws and would-be thieves. As well, Begbie's presence on the creeks was a great satisfaction to those who "had heretofore felt beyond the pale of the law and protection and completely at the mercy of a few drunken desperadoes!"

51

The *Cariboo Sentinel* of August 17, 1863, remarked on the peacefulness of the creeks: "Everything is very quiet and orderly on the creek owing in great measure to Mr. O'Reilly's [the magistrate] efficiency and the wholesome appearance of Judge Begbie who seems to be a terror to evil doers and a sworn enemy to the use of the knife and revolver." Begbie's admonitions to the accused and to juries have become legend.

In one instance, a jury brought in a verdict of manslaughter and Begbie roared at the accused, "Had the jury performed their duty I might now have the painful satisfaction of condemning you to death, and you, gentlemen of the jury, you are a pack of Dallas horse thieves, and permit me to say, it would give me great pleasure to see you hanged, each and every one of you, for declaring a murderer guilty only of manslaughter."

By way of balance, Begbie also charged a man who had pleaded guilty to "Go, and sin no more." He had a great sense of drama. When a dispute arose over a mining claim, he played the role of King Solomon and set up a foot race for the protagonists, from Richfield to the claim. The first man to run the distance and drive in his claim stake was declared winner. In another instance, to avoid nationalistic trouble, he swore in a jury from the country of the accused and let them judge their own (which could be the reason for such results as murderers being found guilty only of manslaughter). Without a doubt, though, Begbie was almost singlehandedly responsible for the sense of law which prevailed in the gold creeks of Cariboo.

Begbie became chief justice of British Columbia in 1870 and was knighted in 1875. Sir Matthew Baillie Begbie died in Victoria on June 11, 1894.

The Nason Family

Ithiel Blake Nason was born in Maine, U.S.A., April 24, 1839, and as a young man swallowed the lure of California gold. In 1858 he drifted north to the Fraser River and turned to another occupation, operating a sawmill at Yale for Jerome and Thaddeus Harper. In 1861 he arrived on Antler Creek with enough money to allow him time to prospect. Near Wolfe Creek he sank three shafts with moderate success. Within a few years, Antler was waning and the sawmill there was put up for sale. Nason and W.A. Meacham bought the equipment and had it moved to Williams Creek, where miners constantly needed lumber—not only for buildings but for the miles of flumes and sluices that crisscrossed the creeks.

Business boomed and the two partners upgraded their operation to a steam sawmill. The *Cariboo Sentinel* of August 27, 1866, carried their announcement: "Williams Creek Sawmill Company. The undersigned lumber merchants beg to inform the inhabitants in general of Williams Creek that they have now in operation a Steam Saw Mill located at the mouth of Mink Gulch above Richfield, capable of manufacturing 1000 feet of lumber per hour, any length, any width required in the market, and of a Superior Quality. All orders left with Mr. W.A. Meacham at Barkerville, or the mill, will be promptly attended to and delivered Free of Charge at any point on the wagon road and at Reduced Rates. The undersigned trust to merit a liberal share of the public patronage and that their old friends will kindly give

At the mouth of Stout's Gulch, Nason's sawmill provided lumber for flumes and buildings. Like most machinery of the period, it was water powered. 1865 photo by Charles Gentile. PABC #95331

them a call. MEACHAM, COOMBS & NASON."

In 1870 the partnership dissolved, but Nason carried on. He also kept an interest in mining as one of the six original shareholders in the Waverley Hydraulic Mining Company, continued work on his two Williams Creek claims (on one of which, The Deadwood, the mill was located), and began a new mill on Jack of Clubs Creek.

In 1875 he married Mary A. Watson in Victoria and began a family of eight children at their home in Richfield. Nason was a member of the Board of Directors of the Cariboo Hospital for 15 years, a school trustee for six and in 1889 was elected to the Legislative Assembly in Victoria. In 1891 he was re-elected in a by-election caused by the death of Barkerville merchant Joe Mason. During his fourth year in office, on May 27, 1893, Nason died of cancer in Victoria. His widow and children moved from Cariboo to Victoria, but this was not to end the Nason influence along Williams Creek.

In 1904 Oliver and Blake Nason, two of Ithiel Nason's sons, returned to Barkerville, where they worked at various mines until enlisting to serve in World War I. Oliver returned in 1932 with his wife Lillian, as did Blake, and again they mined at various sites such as Beggs Gulch and Canadian Creek. Oliver Nason was also hydraulic foreman for the Lowhee Company for a time. In 1955 he was admitted to Shaughnessy Hospital; the family moved to Vancouver and later to Vernon, where on March 1, 1959, Oliver Nason passed away.

Andrew and Elizabeth Kelly

Andrew Kelly, born 1835 in Glasgow, Scotland, apprenticed as a baker then left his home for the gold rush in Ballarat, Australia, at the age of 16. In 1861 he went to California and then to Cariboo, arriving on Antler Creek in 1862 and in the late fall crossed Bald Mountain to the new strikes on Williams Creek.

Elizabeth Kelly. PABC   *Andrew Kelly. PABC*

He intended digging for gold, but in the thousands of miners and the raw new town he saw a greater opportunity and returned to his trade of baker to fill the stomachs of hungry miners. By 1863 he had not only a bakeshop but an establishment called the Wake-Up Jake Bakeshop, Coffee Saloon, and Lunch House. As bread and bannock came from the ovens, so gold came from his claim and although not rich he was soon well established.

Kelly, now a successful businessman, married Elizabeth Hastie, of Ayrshire, Scotland, in Victoria in March 1866 and brought her to the goldfields. Mrs. Kelly later remembered that, "the only difficulty I experienced on that long walk, which was really my honeymoon trip, was during the last 12 miles. We struck a snow storm and my high heels sunk away down, and hoops would keep bobbing up to my shoulders. The latter being such a nuisance that I asked my husband to let the six miners who were sharing the trail with us go ahead a bit. Then I took off my crinoline, and after folding it carried it on my arm. The Scotch plaid which was my mother's parting gift when I left home for California four years previously kept me warm."

The Kellys continued operating the Wake-Up Jake for a few months before selling to Robert Patterson and John G. Goodson in order to follow the Grouse Creek rush that came on the heels of the Heron Claim success. At Grouse Creek they built a boarding house and bakery, which opened on July 22, 1869. Again Kelly operated an adjoining mining claim.

When Grouse Creek gold waned, the Kellys moved back to Barkerville and in 1871 bought the "Kelly Hotel." They had eight children, but their family, like so many others in the 1800s, suffered loss, two children being buried in the Barkerville cemetery. Mrs. Kelly recalled, "I had eight children, and I knitted every stocking they wore. I made their clothes. My husband kept a hotel and restaurant...and I did all the washing and housekeeping."

Mary Hastie, Mrs. Kelly's sister, also came to Barkerville. In 1873, a few years after arriving, she married Thomas Fletcher, who ran a second hand store in town.

Sadness met the family with the murder of their son James A. Kelly in 1904. The 33-year-old man was bludgeoned to death by an Indian woman in a Barkerville cabin.

Mrs. Kelly was also nurse and midwife to the men and women of the creek; in 30 years the Kellys never left Barkerville. Then in the early 1900s they bought a home and retired to Victoria. When Andrew died on August 1, 1923, Elizabeth's chestnut hair went white. "I had dark hair until that time," she said. Elizabeth died on January 9, 1927.

The Chinese

Gum Sahn the Chinese called North America, "Gold Mountain," a literal translation of the Chinese characters that now represent this continent. The lure of wealth brought people to any gold rush, and the Chinese were no exception. Their first introduction in historic times was the California gold rush. They came from poor farms to a land that was, in their eyes, uncivilized, populated by "Barbarians" and "round-eyes." They came with pride in their ancient, rich culture which had bloomed while most Europeans were still living in caves. Chinese heritage included a language, customs, traditions and knowledge that in many instances surpassed that of Western civilization and certainly that of rough, crude North Americans.

Chinese who left Kwungtung province for the new land were called Gold Mountain men. Poems and songs were sung about them:

If you have a daughter, don't marry her to a Gold Mountain boy.
Out of ten years, he will not be in bed for even one.
The spider spins webs on top of the bed.
While dust covers fully one side of the bed.

To the whites of California and British Columbia, they were "Celestials," "slant-eyes," "Chinees," "Chinks" and, in the view of most miners, came only to take the gold and rush back to China as wealthy men. In their desire to find gold, the Chinese were little different from most miners, who came not to settle but to tear out the gold and retreat. The Chinese dealt with these cultural and racial conflicts by forming associations of friends and neighbors called tongs and by keeping a low profile when it came to mining.

The British government encouraged Chinese immigration to British Columbia, aiding large merchants like the Kwong Lee Company to import indentured laborers from the poorer provinces of China—a system similar to the Hudson's Bay Company's importation of young Scots to serve in the fur trade. Chinese immigration presented

This painting by Overlander William G. Hind shows Chinese miners at work on the Fraser in 1862.

the government with a body of easily-controlled people who helped offset the enormous influx of Americans, who might make a move toward annexation by occupation. In turn, the Chinese preferred what they called the British government's "square and equal rule" to Californian influence on Williams Creek. An example of Chinese preference for British rule was seen at a Fraser Canyon Cariboo Road toll gate, operated by a Chinese. He posted a notice that "King George Men" were to pay one price and "Boston Men," Americans, double.

At the same time, Governor Douglas, taken aback by the influx of thousands of Chinese from California to the Fraser River rush, wrote: "They are certainly not a desirable class of people, as a permanent population, but are for the present useful as labourers, and, as consumers, of a revenue-paying character."

Judge Begbie took a different tack: "The Chinese are here. There is nothing in British Constitution to say they should not be, and while they are here we should protect them as we would any white man, and sometimes better."

Robert Stevenson, John "Cariboo" Cameron's partner, said of the Chinese, "they were kept out of Cariboo until the fall of 1864, when a Chinese cook who was with Jack Bowie's pack train got a foothold in Barkerville. After that it was simply impossible to keep them out, as the law protected them like any other human being."

While Stevenson's dates are inaccurate for Cariboo generally, they could be correct for Barkerville. More importantly he illustrates the racist sentiments of his day. In 1862 over 1000 Chinese worked on the construction of the Cariboo Road, and by 1861 Chinese were already being hired to augment the Antler Creek labor force.

The Chinese in North American tended to settle in village groups or clans. Records show, for example, that 77 percent of Quesnellemouth Chinese came from K'ai-p'ing. Of the population of 400, over half were Chou's from K'ai-p'ing.

In Barkerville the Chinese formed a large and important segment of the community. They did not restrict themselves to laboring jobs. Many saw this new land as an opportunity to move ahead and formed the new merchant class, the social elite of the new world. And although Chinatown was their business center, Chinese shops were scattered along the length of the creek. Chinese merchants in the north end of town lost heavily during the Great Fire of 1868, but most of Chinatown (at the south end) survived and retained the character of the pre-fire town: crowded, dirty and unsafe.

While a few Chinese women came to the mining grounds, they were the exception. The fare to the new world was prohibitive, and the Chinese commitment to family, clan and village remained strong. The men intended to return to support this connection with gold. This commitment, and later the immigration restrictions and head tax, resulted in a primarily bachelor society.

By the close of the 1870s, most mining ground was either in the hands of large companies, or individuals who patiently worked small claims. Unemployment became a problem. And the Chinese, though they struck for higher wages in Barkerville, were still being paid only one-half to two-thirds the wage of white miners. Sentiments against Orientals increased with unemployment. But scattered along the gold creeks of B.C., Chinese mined and garden, smoked a little opium (legal until 1908) and lived their solitary bachelor lives.

The next decade was a difficult one for immigrants, relieved only by work on the transcontinental railways and the vast labor force required. By the end of construction the Chinese population of British Columbia was over 20,000. Over half the population of Cariboo was Chinese. Quesnelleforks, Dog Creek and other camps were over 95 percent Chinese. By now the B.C. government was charging Chinese $10 per year for a licence to live in the province. In 1884 a head tax of $50 was levied on immigrants. It was raised to $100 in 1900 and $500 in 1903. No other immigrant group has had to pay a similar tax. The 1924 Asian exclusion act barred all Chinese, except consuls, merchants and students. The act was repealed in 1947, but not until 1966, 109 years after the first Chinese miners arrived at Fort Victoria, were nationality and race removed as criteria for selecting immigrants.

Gold Rush Music

Barkerville was a noisy town with its cacophonous blend of mechanical and animal sounds. The creek rushed; the Cornish wheels thumped and squeaked; wagon wheels crunched in gravel; animals bellowed, neighed and barked; blacksmiths' shops echoed with the clang of metal being worked; doors slammed; men shouted; skirts rustled; and from the many saloons came the sounds of the fiddle, concertina, piano, cornet and a variety of other brass and stringed instruments. Barkerville was making music.

When men and women left their homes for a new land, they brought a few items to remind them of a home they might never see again and that might help pass some of the lonely, weary hours. As a young traveller of today might throw a guitar over her shoulder or stick a harmonica in his pocket, so the gold rush men and women brought their musical instruments to the creeks.

Instruments that were popular in the 1860s and that were recorded in Barkerville are those easily carried—the fiddle, guitar, banjo, cornet, clarinet, concertina, flute, bombardon and tin whistle. As families established roots, the most popular instruments of the day—the piano, harmonium and organ—were brought in. Many are the tales of men who packed a particular piano over some mountain trail. Parlor music was a family's most common entertainment, with an occasional outing to a church concert or the Theatre Royal.

In saloons and the theatre, popular music was played, songs such as "The Old Oaken Bucket," "Dixie Land," "Yellow Rose of Texas," "Castles in the Air," and "Maggie May," as well as the many songs of Stephen Foster that often went with a minstrel show. James Anderson the poet wrote local songs, and miners brought songs from the California rush written by "Old Put" and tunes from Australia that told mining stories and folklore.

Then there were the songs of the homeland, the Scottish and Irish tunes, the patriotic British hymns such as "Rule Britannia," "Men of Harlech" or the "British Grenadiers" and at every concert, "God Save the Queen." St. Saviour's Church Institute, begun by the Reverend Reynard, quickly became an important focal point for town musicians. The frequent concerts were social highlights for the town.

For a miner, an institute concert began with a hike to town and a visit to a bath house to remove not only the grime of a mine but some of the aches gathered along the way. Then came dinner at the Jake or a saloon and a leisurely stroll down the board walk to St. Saviour's to enjoy a "Benefit For The Town Band." Tickets were $1, $1.50 for a reserved seat.

Outside St. Saviour's Church a piper might play a gathering tune as the audience filed in, men doffing their hats, ladies nodding to acquaintances, smiling and greeting friends. A lonely single miner took what little comfort he could from this all-too-infrequent sight of women, hoping for an introduction to a lady in the choir.

A *Sentinel* announcement for a Saturday evening concert included:
Quick March—"Gruss am Breslan."
Selection of Welsh Melodies—"Men of Harlech," "The Ash Grove" and "The Boat Song"

Chorus—"See our Oars"
Quartette—The Minstrel Boy"
Magic Lantern Pictures, interspersed with music.
Glee—"The Witches"
Cornet solo—Mr. Elder, "Melodies from La Traviata"
Ballad—Mrs. Brown, "Bonnie Nellie Brown"
March—"Old Folks at Home"
Song—Mr. Powell, "The Boy at Biscay."
Quartette for Stringed Instruments—1st violin, Mr. Scott; 2nd
    violin, Mr. Elder; viola, Mr. Reynard; violincello, Mr. Powell
Ballad—"Good-bye Sweetheart"
Chorus—"I See Them On Their Winding Way"
Ballad—Mr. Gomer Johns Chorus, "When Winds Breath Soft"
Selections of Scotch Melodies—"Scots wha hae," "Land o' the
    Leal," "Banks and Braes," "Auld Acquaintance," "Yellow
    Haired Laddie"
"Rule Britannia"
GOD SAVE THE QUEEN

The concert ended, people made their way home with friends. A
few men headed for Fanny's newest saloon and a lone miner waited
outside for the choir to leave. He saw a certain lady greet another man,
a merchant, and he walked up the boardwalk alone. This was
Barkerville, 1871.

*Jason Young and Ralph Scoullar (as editor Robert Holloway) tend the
presses of the* Cariboo Sentinel.

Newspaper Pioneers

The founder of Barkerville's *Cariboo Sentinel,* George Wallace, first
appeared on the British Columbia scene in 1862 as a Toronto *Globe*
correspondent with the Overlanders' party. Wallace went to Victoria at
the end of the trek, where he tried to start a new weekly called *The
Globe.* This venture failed without an issue's being printed, so he joined

the *British Colonist* staff. In the spring of 1863 he and Charles W. Allen launched the *Daily Evening Express* which published from April 26, 1863, to February 12, 1865, and vigorously promoted the union of the separate colonies of British Columbia and Vancouver Island.

Wallace then left his partner to run the paper and headed north to Cariboo where on August 9, 1863, he received Free-miner's Certificate #65 and became a partner in the Aurora claim. On April 5, 1865, the *Colonist* reported on Wallace's return to journalism: "Cariboo Newspaper. The steamer *Enterprise* carried up yesterday morning a printing press, and part of the regular material for a newspaper, which is about to be established at Williams Creek, Cariboo, by Mr. George Wallace, formerly of the *Evening Express*. The name of the new journal is to be the *Cariboo Express*. The press was supplied from the *Colonist* office."

The press George Wallace used to publish the *Cariboo Sentinel* (the name *Express* was never used) came to Barkerville with its own history. It was originally owned by the Society for the Propagation of the Gospel of Paris and had been sent with its archaic French type to do similar service in California. In 1856 it was shipped up the coast to Roman Catholic Bishop Demers at Victoria. It was the first press west of the Great Lakes in British North America. When the gold rush hit the colonies in 1858, the *Vancouver Island Gazette* printed on the rented Demers press. But the *Gazette* published only eight issues, and when Demers tried to found a French newspaper it lasted only two issues.

Demers sold the press to Amor De Cosmos who used it to found the *British Colonist*. And in 1863 Amor De Cosmos sold the press to George Wallace, who brought it north, in pieces, on men's backs, over the mountain trails to the new town of Barkerville.

The Victoria *Colonist* Amor De Cosmos sold for 12.5 cents or one bit, while the Barkerville *Sentinel* was a costly $1. Still, miners eagerly awaited the *Sentinel*. The circulation was about 500, and it was later reported that the advertisements were a "mine of wealth." Wallace was content with one season's profits of $3500, and in 1866 he sold to Alexander Allan and Warren Lambert.

Allan was not as successful with the *Sentinel* as Wallace. Two years after buying the paper, he wrote a bitter letter to his mother explaining that his poor circumstances were the result of the paper.

I have for the last 2 years owned and conducted the first newspaper ever published in these extreme north western settlements...but it has not been a source of profit to me, on the contrary it has been a constant source of annoyance and expense and I am only too glad that I have managed to sell out of it a few weeks ago. My intention is now to resume mining by which ere the season closes I hope to realize sufficient means to enable me to pay a visit to the old sod once more.

My newspaper enterprise has not been fraught with profit to me, tho' I have worked and slaved both night and day for the last two years even at the expense of my health...even now when I have concluded a sale of the business the sum I receive will not extricate me from the debts I owe. If I could collect all that is due to me I should be clear with the world, and in a more prosperous condition than I have been since the disastrous years of 1864 & 65 which plunged me into difficulties I am now trying to extricate myself from. Had I been inclined to use the means that were open to me then I might have got clear from all my debts amounting to many hundred dollars by going thro' the Bankruptcy Court but this course I scorned to adopt.

Allan obviously had troubles. Another letter of January 1870 bemoans his "misfortune, disappointment and lack of opportunity" and goes on to describe his continued bad luck and the recession that was affecting Barkerville. Times and work were hard. Allan was not able to stand the gaff.

After Allan, The *Cariboo Sentinel* continued under various editors—including John McLaren, buried in the Barkerville cemetery—for several years. The last editor-proprietor was another Overlander of '62 named Robert Holloway. Holloway's wife joined him in Victoria soon after he came out. In 1864 they had a daughter and in 1869 a son. Holloway journeyed to Cariboo in 1865 as a prospector but chose to winter more comfortably with his wife and children in Victoria. In 1868 he bought the *Cariboo Sentinel* from "Wallace and Dearburg," indicating that Wallace may have retained some interest when he sold to Allan and Lambert. Holloway had no sooner taken over than the office was destroyed by the Great Fire of 1868. By some accounts Holloway then moved the paper to Richfield. When the *Cariboo Sentinel* folded in 1875, Holloway moved to Victoria where he worked for the *Colonist* and later for the provincial government. He died in 1909.

George Wallace's life after the *Cariboo Sentinel* was decidedly more interesting than Holloway's. After selling out in 1866 he was elected to the Legislative Assembly and brought machinery from San Francisco to begin a newspaper in the Columbia River's Big Bend Country, site of a gold rush. The newspaper failed, but he did eventually publish *The British Columbia Tribune* at Yale for a season, leaving "in conse-quence of pressing business of a private nature...in the old country."

Wallace's next employment was a long step for a Cariboo newspaper editor. In Japan he contracted to manage "The Great Dragon Troupe" of native acrobats and jugglers. This evidently brought him profits of over half a million dollars. A few years later he conducted the celebrated Siamese Twins on a similar tour, for similar profits. Wallace then settled in London, married and had two sons. In 1881 he was back in Canada as a journalist, his wife having died a few years previously. His obituary in the *Montreal Star* of May 19, 1887, said he had died about 10 days before, "having never recovered from the shock of his wife's death." He was, it said, "universally respected" and "left many friends."

The little Demers press that Wallace had used to found the *Cariboo Sentinel* churned out newspapers on Williams Creek and elsewhere for many years after Wallace, Allan and Holloway left Barkerville. It survived the fire of 1868 and then went to Richfield for 10 years. Later the press was used in Yale and Kamloops to print the *Inland Sentinel*. The press was retired in 1887 when it went to the Sisters of St. Anne of Kamloops, who later placed it in their Victoria convent museum.

Medical Care and the Royal Cariboo Hospital

Digging Cariboo gold was hard, dangerous work, and miners suffered a variety of ailments, from fractures and heart attacks to diarrhoea and syphilis. Doctors followed miners to the creeks and did their best in what was still a primitive science to alleviate suffering. However, there was no place for doctors to practice and patients to recuperate. Barkerville and Cameronton had barely been born when a typhoid epidemic, caused in part by poor sanitation practices, raged up and down Williams Creek.

Miner John Morris wrote: *Sickness is very prevalent throughout the creek; a dangerous fever has broke out amongst us and carried off several of our fellows. There is no provision yet made for the indigent sick; an hospital is much required.*

In response to the typhoid, lumped with other illnesses under "mountain fever," a public meeting on July 22, 1863, resolved that a hospital was "imperatively demanded."

At the time, such care was not considered government responsibility, so miners sold subscriptions for a hospital. A week later a design and location were decided on. The location was in Marysville, on the creek's east side below Cameronton. In August Judge Begbie and Gold Commissioner O'Reilly laid the foundation and on October 1st, the "dingy, quaint-looking log cabin" institution was opened. The Williams Creek Hospital consisted of one ward, a doctor's office and a kitchen. It was several years before a bathroom was added.

While several doctors had private practices on the creek, Dr. Walter Shaw Black, who had trained in London and come to Cariboo from the Australia rushes, was appointed as hospital surgeon.

In the first nine months 32 men were admitted. By July 1st, 26 had been discharged, three had died and three remained in hospital. But already the facility was in debt by a third of its budget.

Hospital board chairman James Wattie, an Overlander, appealed to Governor Seymour for a bailout and $6000 a year for future operation. Newspapers editorials asked how the hospital could continue without government support, suggesting that Cariboo miners were heavy tax contributors and therefore should be given financial support.

But miners did not sit back and wait for government grants to roll in. They held a concert and ball to raise more funds. After much negotiation and several months, the government in Victoria agreed to a yearly grant of $6000.

The hospital experienced more than its share of troubles. It was always scrambling for funds, often in debt. Surgeons commonly had to wait months to be paid and often volunteered. There were charges of misappropriation of funds, incorrect billing, mismanagement, incompetence and arguments between the surgeon in charge and the board.

In 1891 the Marysville site was abandoned and a new hospital built on the old Cariboo Road above Cameronton, a site now marked with a cairn. It was called the Royal Cariboo Hospital and operated until 1925, when it closed for ten years.

In 1934 a new society formed to reopen the hospital in response to the Wells mining boom. The resurrection was short-lived. On March 29, 1936, the hospital burned to the ground. It was not replaced. Instead, a hospital was opened in Wells. It has since closed.

Fred Ludditt - Barkerville's Champion

Fred Ludditt came to Barkerville for the second gold rush in the 1930s and stayed until the outbreak of World War II. He came to stake a few claims in May 1945 and returned in the fall with his wife Esther. They planned to stay one winter. There are many people who come to these creeks for one month, one winter, one year. Few leave quickly. Fred and Esther stayed for 18 years, and in later life often returned for the summer.

More than anyone else, Fred Ludditt was responsible for Barkerville's preservation and restoration. In the summer of 1947, Ludditt watched as the original Government Assay Office was torn down, a building "of inestimable worth historically" Ludditt called it. The same year, the John Hopp Office was torn down. This was originally Scott's Saloon, one of the few buildings to survive the fire of 1868, and it contained many precious old records. Then Tommy Blair's store went, and the Hudson's Bay Company store, with years of records. Chinese building were ripped apart and used for firewood, and souvenir hunters ransacked the town and the cemeteries.

In response to this destruction, Fred Ludditt formed the Barkerville Historic and Development Company in 1953. Gradually, with the support of many—including pioneers such as Lottie Bowron, Ralph Chetwynd, Minister of Trade and Industry, Cariboo MLA Bill Speare and Governor General Vincent Massey—the value of Barkerville was recognized. When British Columbia Centennial celebrations and projects were initiated prior to 1958, the seeds for a rebirth of Barkerville had been sown. The Wells-Barkerville Centennial Committee was formed, and a booklet by Fred Ludditt called *Gold in the Cariboo* was published. (It is still available and is filled with interesting stories.)

The British Columbia Centennial was the catalyst that Barkerville needed. Articles and stories were published by the dozen; visitors came by the hundreds. "Suddenly," Fred Ludditt wrote, "there seemed to be *too many* visitors." Ludditt viewed this new interest in Barkerville ironically, after his early unsupported years, but it was his dogged persistence that had finally "struck the lead." In 1958 the provincial government declared Barkerville a historic park and began stabilization and restoration.

The first reconstructive years were not without problems, disappointments, misunderstandings and a lack of sensitivity. To Ludditt's chagrin, the restoration often did not proceed as he and other oldtimers had planned. There was little communication between Parks Branch staff and the originators of the restoration, resulting in frayed tempers and, in some cases, permanent hostility. However, as Ludditt himself said, there was "much to offset these disappointments and create for the visitor a feeling of having stepped behind the curtain of time into surroundings and sights of more than a century ago."

KEY TO BUILDING
LOCATIONS

Walk-in Displays
Operating Business
Original pre-1900 Building
Washroom ♦♦
Outdoor Toilet Ⓣ
Limited Wheelchair
accessibility

1. Administration Building
2. The Gold Rush Diner
   (Refreshment Stand)
2a. Washrooms in Parking Lot ♦♦
3. Aurora Claim Cabin and Cornish
   Wheel
4. Eldorado Gold Panning and
   Souvenirs
5. Tregillus Family Buildings
6. Visitor Interpretation Center
   (Admissions, Security and First-aid)
   Entrance to Heritage Area
7. Watchmakers Shop
8. Westleyan Methodist Church
9. Miners Boarding House
10. St. Saviour's Anglican
    Church

Richfield 1.6 km

N

Flume

Bulkhead

Williams Creek

0   15   30   45   60
Metres

93   94

Pedestrian
Bridge

BARKERVILLE
HISTORIC TOWN

A WALKING TOUR OF
WILLIAMS CREEK

Barkerville's town planning was initially dictated by gold mining. The gold lay hidden in ice-age gravels. As it was discovered and torn from the earth, miners' humble homes, tents and rude cabins sprang up on the 100-foot-square claims. When there were enough miners to need supplies, merchants arrived. As a permanent community developed, tents gave way to log buildings. Soon an entrepreneur built a mill supplying lumber for flumes, shaft houses and stores.

Early planning was based on staked claim lines and natural terrain. Gold dictated the location of shaft houses and Cornish water wheels, water the route of flumes. While cabins, tents, warehouses and some flumes perched on the side hills, topography confined larger buildings to the bottom of the narrow, steep-walled valley, forced into the creek channel in a rough, straggling line. Flat land was at a premium, more so then than now, for mining refuse has since raised the creek bed an estimated 30 feet.

11. Williams Creek School House
12. William Bowron House
13. Wendle House (Domestic)
14. Cameron & Ames' Blacksmith Shop
15. Barnard's Express (Theatre Royal tickets sold here)
16. Barkerville Bakery
17. Post Office (Full Postal Services)
18. J.P. Taylor Drugstore
19. Masonic Hall (Meetings 2nd Saturday April - December)
20. Joe Denny's Saloon
21. House Hotel (Rootbeer Saloon)
22. Carriage Shed
23. Mason and Daly General Store
24. C. Strouss General Merchants
25. Carriage Shed
26. Van Volkenburgh Cabin
27. Barker Co. Flume (Future Reconstruction)
28. Cariboo Sentinel Print Shop

29. Mrs. Neate's House (Dressmaker)
30. Kerr's Phoenix Brewery ♥♥
31. Johnny Knott's Carpenter Shop
32. Kwong Lee Wing Kee Manager's House
33. Water Pipes
34. Kibbee House (Original New England Bakery)
35. Wa Lee Store
36. Yan War Store
37. Ming Yee Tong
38. Kwong Sang Wing Store (Archeology Display)
39. Miners Cabin
40. Mrs. Houser's House
41. Site of Later Barker Co. Shaft
42. Sing Kee Herbalist
43. Gee Quon (Residence)
44. Lee Chong's Store
45. Chee Kung Tong (Chinese Masonic Hall)
46a. Tai Ping Fong (Peace Room)
46b. Dannhauer/Halverson House
47. Lung Duck Tong (Chinese Restaurant)
48. Sporting House

49. The Clearing (Site of Special Events)
50. Flagpole (for greasy pole climb on Special Events Days)
51. Havelock Cabin
52. Site of the original Barker Co. Discovery Shaft
53. Sandy MacArthur's Blacksmith Shop
54. Firehall
55. Theatre Royal
56. Barkerville Hotel
57. Kelly General Store
58. Kelly Saloon
59. Government Assay Office
60. Sin Hap Laundry
61. Louis Wilde Bootmaker
62. Louis A. Blanc (Photographic Gallery)
63. Dr. Jones' Dentist Office
64. St. George Saloon (Staff Facility)
65. Mme. Bendixon's Saloon & Boarding House
66. Dr. Hugh Watts' Office and Residence
67. Moses' Barbershop
68. Wake-Up-Jake Restaurant & Coffee Saloon
69. J.H Todd General Store

70. Wilfred Thompson House
71. Gold Commissioners Office & Library
72. McIntyre House (Staff Facility)
73. John Bowron House
74. Bibby's Tin Shop
75. King House (Staff Facility)
76. McLeod Cabin
77. Holt & Burgess Cabinet Maker's Shop
78. W. Baker Stables
79. Mundorf Stables
80. BX Express (Stagecoach Rides)
81. Kelly House (Staff Facility)
82. Display Studio (Staff Facility)
83. Michael Claim Cabin
84. Lowhee Cabin (Staff Facility)
85. Hibernia Claim Cabin
86. Sheepskin Mining Co. Shaft
87. Sheepskin Mining Co. Cabin
88. Chinese Miners Cabin
89. Trapper Dan's Cabin
90. Eagle Claim Cornish Wheel
91. Eagle Claim Cabin
92. Flume
93. Gunn Claim Hydraulic Mining Pit
94. Canadian Claim Tunnel and Adit
95. Keystone Drill (Future Restoration)
96. Sawmill (Future Restoration)
97. Stampmill (Future Restoration)

The first surveys were by the Royal Engineers in the summer of 1863, one year after buildings first sprouted beside the creek. Sergeant William McColl, R.E., began work along Williams Creek July 11, 1863, beginning south or upstream of Richfield and continuing north to the downstream end of Cameronton. He surveyed the creek and staked three townsites while Lance Corporal J. Turnbull, R.E., plotted the sites. Their plans show lots, building fronts, some shafts, streams, the toe of the bluff and Williams Creek meandering as far into town as the site of the Theatre Royal. Since the three towns existed before the survey, the engineer's task was to fit the random locations of existing buildings into a semblance of regular lots. The topography that had restricted building aided this plotting.

In Barkerville there were 40 buildings on 61 lots. Richfield, a few miles upstream, had 43 buildings on 76 lots, and Cameronton, a few miles downstream, had 37 buildings on 73 lots.

Where Sergeant McColl was not confined by existing buildings, he drew a standard lot with a 60-foot frontage and 132-foot depth. Lots were sold based on this plan. McColl's survey numbers are now referred to as "Old Survey" lots. A 1933 "New Survey," which renumbered and reallocated, is used today.

Beyond this survey, town planning was almost non-existent. The result was an absence of cross streets, a narrow, inefficient main street, a random growth of buildings and generally crowded, unsanitary conditions. Added to these problems was a creek that ran through the town, natural hillside seepage that almost gave the town the name of Springfield and mining refuse that threatened to bury the buildings. This combination of handicaps led to a unique response. Buildings and sidewalks were supported by pilings or stilts that could be jacked up ahead of the rising tailings.

Domestic water was provided by springs in the western hillside, fed to water troughs by hollowed wooden pipes. Sewage and garbage disposal service did not exist, all refuse going into the nearest abandoned shaft or a hole dug in the gravel. This made the creek water unfit to drink and was the cause of the 1863 typhoid epidemic. One positive outcome of this epidemic was the construction of the Royal Cariboo Hospital.

Barkerville and Cameronton boomed and caused one reporter for the *Colonist* to remark that Barkerville was "fast becoming the largest city west of Chicago and North of San Francisco." It is one of the popular myths of Cariboo history that Barkerville *was* the largest city west of Chicago and North of San Francisco. Not so, as a glance at photos of St. Paul, Minnesota; Portland, Oregon; Port Townsend, Washington; Victoria or even Quesnelle Forks will confirm. In 1867 one of the few accounts of Barkerville buildings was published. The writer remarked that most of the principal buildings of Cameronton "have been removed to Barkerville." New buildings were going up, but the count for spring of 1867 was: 12 saloons, 10 stores, 3 shoemakers, 3 restaurants, 3 lodging houses, 2 banks, 2 drug stores, 2 watchmakers, 2 breweries, 2 tin shops, 2 blacksmiths, 1 express office, 2 carpenter shops, 1 post office, 1 printing office, 1 public library, 1 paint shop, 1 clothing store, 1 butcher's stall and 1 public stable. Not a building site was left unoccupied.

The crowded, unplanned town gave more cautious citizens cause for alarm. There was a fire company, but the tightly packed buildings left no fire lanes in a town where land was too valuable to "waste." A stage driver described Barkerville townsite as: "Buildings shoulder to shoulder, stovepipes shoved thru flimsy roofs at crazy angles—not even a barrel of water—no insurance. ..."

The summer of 1868 was long, hot and dry. The town was a pile of tinder. Photographer Frederick Dally was worried. He often thought about fire. On the night of September 15 he sat and watched a spectacular display of the *Aurora borealis*.

Whilst viewing this grand spectacle my attention was drawn to the town...where dancing and revelry was going on, by the number of stovepipes very close together coming through the wooden roofs of the buildings at every height and in every direction that were sending forth myriads of sparks. Numbers of them were constantly alighting on the roofs where they would remain many seconds before going out and from the dryness of the season I came to the conclusion that unless we shortly had rain or snow to cover the roofs...the town was doomed.

When I mentioned the probability of a fire to the businessmen of the place they answered me...that the wood the town was built of was different to other wood and that it would not burn...so they remained passive in their fancied security and had nothing done to guard against so dire a calamity.

The morning was bright and clear and the sluice boxes bore traces of a hard frost as the icicles were two or three yards in length by several feet in depth looking very beautiful. The business of the day commenced. A young man, Patterson...showed me over his large and well built premises containing a large stock of goods...all paid for.

September 16th was windy. Sam Drake was working the dump box of the Wake-Up Jake claim when he heard a woman scream. "I looked up," he said, "to see smoke pouring through the roof of the dance hall. I called to the men, who came running. ..."

Photographer Dally wrote, *I heard several [people] running on the plank sidewalk and heard one exclaim, 'Good God, what is up!' I ran instantly to see the cause of the alarm and to my astonishment beheld a column of smoke rising from the roof of the saloon adjoining the steward's house. I saw the fire had a firm hold and as there was no water to be had I felt certain that the town would be destroyed, so I collected as much of my stock of goods as possible together, and hastened with them to the middle of the creek.*

The fire originated in a small room adjoining Barry & Adlers Saloon...and in no less than two minutes the whole saloon was in flames which quickly set the opposite business, the Bank of British North America, in flames, so the fire travelled at the same time up and down the sides of the street, as fast against the fire as before it. Although my building was nearly fifty yards away from where the fire originated in less than twenty minutes it, together with the whole of the lower part of the town was a sheet of fire, hissing, crackling and roaring furiously.

There was in a store not far from my place fifty kegs of blasting powder and had that not been removed at the commencement of the fire, and put down a dry shaft, most likely not a soul would have been left alive. Blankets and bedding were seen to be sent at least 200 feet high when a number of coal oil tins (5 gallons) exploded. The top of one of the tins was sent five miles and dropped at the sawmill on Grouse Creek.

Every person was thinking of his own property and using desperate efforts to save it, and some not placing it sufficiently far out of reach of the element had all consumed, and others had taken it so far that during the time they were away trying to save more property Chinamen and others were stealing from them as fast as they could carry it away.

The town was divided by the "Barker" flume crossing it at a height of about fifty feet, and as it was carrying all the water that was near, it kept the fire at bay for a short time from the upper part of the town, but the hot wind soon drove those that were standing on it away. The fire then quickly caught the other half of the buildings, also the forest on the mountain ridge at the back. As the sun set behind the mountain...the cold frosty wind came sweeping down the canyon blowing without sympathy on the houseless and distressed sufferers... Household furniture of every description was piled along the side of the creek, and the people were

Shortly before the Great Fire of 1868, Frederick Dally took this photo of a somnolent Barkerville. Note that the Black Jack Cut at the south end of town is not yet begun. VCA #9603

preparing to make themselves as comfortable...as circumstances would allow.

In the early morning as I passed down the creek I saw strong men rise from their hard beds on the cold stones. At a quarter to three p.m. the fire had commenced; at half past four p.m. the whole town was in flames, and at 10 o'clock the next morning the signs of rebuilding had commenced and lumber was fast arriving from the sawmill and selling at $125.00 per one thousand feet. Before the fire it sold for $80.00. The number of houses destroyed was one hundred and sixteen. After the fire I found I had the key of my house in my pocket.

The fire was caused by a miner trying to kiss one of the girls that was ironing, and knocking against the stove displaced the pipe that went through the canvas ceiling, and through the roof, which at once took fire. This information I got from an eye witness who never made it generally known thinking that it might result in a lynching.

When the fire abated one building was left standing near the upper end of town, Scott's Saloon. It was close to the Barker flume, and water had been dumped on it to quench the flame. Most of Chinatown also survived. At the lower end, McInne's Saloon and a couple of warehouses survived. The rest was gone. The losses were staggering:

The day after the fire, Dally photographed the smoking ruins. Already green lumber is piled in the ashes ready to rebuild. PABC #10072

Strouss' Store, $100,000; Hudson's Bay Company, $65,000; N. Cunio, Barkerville Brewery, $4000; Kwong Lee Store, $40,000; F. Castagnette Store, $33,000; Cohen & Hoffman Store, $32,000; Lecuyer & Brun Hotel, $20,000; British North America Bank, $10,000; Masonic Lodge, $4000; and many more small merchants—in all, a total of over half a million dollars.

More tragic were the losses of small businesses and individuals who saw their hopes, hard work and savings disappear in a matter of two hours. A few packed what little was left of their belongings and turned their backs on the town. Those who stayed began immediately, as Dally indicated, to build a new and better-planned town.

The cleared townsite allowed Gold Commissioner Chartres Brew to institute some order. The main street was widened, allowance made for cross streets, and buildings were built a uniform three feet off the ground, a move that helped even out the sidewalks.

By September 22, 1868, less than a week after the fire, 20 buildings were up, with many more under construction, their completion delayed only by a shortage of carpenters and tools. By spring the town was rebuilt and by 1870, the focus year of the present reconstruction, it was a mature community serving several thousand people.

The catastrophic fire of 1868 had instilled in Barkervillians a desire for increased protection. From this grew the Williams Creek

69

Barkerville the morning after the fire. The structure at left is thought to be the Bank of British Columbia's safe. PABC #94701

Fire Brigade, organized by Isaac Oppenheimer. Hoses of buffalo hide, pumps, hose wagons, ladders and hooks for pulling down flaming walls, were purchased by public donation, shipped from San Francisco and stored in the lower floor of the Theatre Royal.

The brigade's water supply was two wooden tanks on the hillside. In their weekly drills brigade members sprayed the roofs of the town with water, their practice sessions serving to allay the danger of sparks and the nuisance of dust.

The Brigade's popularity as a social organization was such that members paid fees to belong and in return had the privilege and honor of parading through town in their attractive scarlet and black military-like uniforms on public holidays.

Another fire precaution was the idea of storekeeper W.W. Dodd, who in April 1871 ran a narrow wooden walkway along the peak of his store roof, accessible by a ladder and stationed with water barrels. The barrels remained full, compliments of the heavy rainfall, and were used to douse sparks from a chimney or nearby fire landing on the highly flammable spruce-shaked roofs.

Because of the precautions and the relative care taken in rebuilding the town, Barkerville was never to know the destruction of another great fire. Despite Brew's planning some owners were reluctant to conform, slow to make their buildings a standard height. Some neglected their buildings altogether, only to find them half buried when they returned from a winter in the south. The regulations soon fell into disuse and irregularities returned.

As Barkerville approached 1870s maturity, it was a town planned and built in response to disaster, epidemic, inconvenience and unimagined wealth. The town's life, though, did not stop in 1870. It suffered periodic ups and downs as fortunes in gold fluctuated. As a mature town it was alive in the 1930s when hardrock mines developed in Wells, and though its fortunes were declining there were still folks living here when it became a historic site in 1958. It was a town unique in Canada, likely in North America, and today stands as an example of ingenuity and determination, of laborious debt and death, and of hard-earned, short-lived wealth.

The Williams Creek Fire Brigade displays its hooks, ladder and hose in front of the firehall and Theatre Royal. John Bowron is standing in the doorway wearing a light hat. VPL #8640

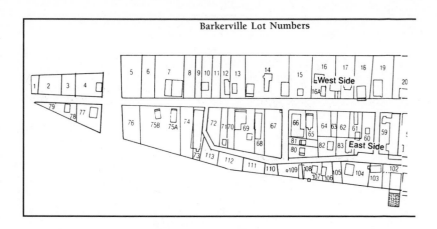

Barkerville Lot Numbers

The Walking Tour

The walking tour of Barkerville, beginning at the visitor reception building, will lead you along Barkerville's Valley of the Flags to the buildings and the stories of people who inhabited the town. The tour begins at the north end of town, moves up the west side, down the east side, then up the back street and over to the bulkhead. This puts you back at the south end ready for a walk to Richfield and a visit with Judge Begbie.

Avoid the tendency to rush. Visit more than once, early in the morning or late in the evening when the town is quiet, when the old residents, Billy Barker, Fanny Bendixon, John Cameron, the Chinese merchants and all the others can best be felt. It is a time of magic.

Barkerville Visitor Reception Centre

The reception centre should be a visitor's first stop. Displays and audiovisual presentations provide a gold rush overview and put Barkerville in its historical perspective. Once you leave this building, interpretation focuses on 1870, when Barkerville was a mature town but when gold fever had died and many merchants were moving.

The curatorial and administrative offices for the site are in the building on the left of the reception centre.

Aurora Claim and Cornish Wheel

The Aurora Company, sometimes known as the Alert Company, was the subject of a dispute with the black-miner-owned Davis Co., which staked nearby ground and struck gold. Judge Cox ruled for the blacks, but the Aurora Co. ignored his decision and dug a shaft. In an appeal Judge Begbie ruled against the blacks, despite all their work.

The El Dorado Shaft House

This modern-day concession fills the needs of 1990s Barkerville visitors just as the general merchants filled miners' needs in the 1800s. Visitors can buy souvenirs, books on the area, or gold. They can also learn the skill of gold panning in the sluice boxes provided. The

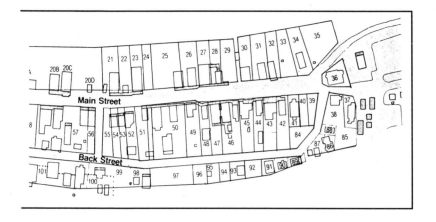

building replicates the size and shape of shaft houses common on the creek. In the 1930s it was a livery stable.

The gold pan was the prospector's basic tool. He used it not only for testing creek gravels, but as a frying pan, a dinner plate, porridge bowl and an oven for bannock. In testing gravel it was used in a simple fashion, based on two principles: first, that a shaking or rocking motion causes gold to settle to the bottom, and second, that water action washes away lighter gravels leaving gold—five times heavier than rock—in the bottom of the pan. These principles served not only the prospector's pan, but the miners' sluices and rockers.

Tregillus Family Buildings

These few buildings are still owned by the Tregillus family. The main house is thought to have been moved here from Reduction Road in 1900. It is unclear whether the outbuildings were built after that time as the need required or if they are older buildings moved in.

Fred Tregillus came in 1886 after mining in other parts of B.C. and actively mined in the Lightning Creek area. In 1905 he married Mary House, daughter of Charles and Margaret House of the House Hotel. He continued mining in the area for many years. Mary Tregillus died in 1947, Fred in August 1962, just short of his 100th birthday.

Wesleyan Methodist Church Lot A

Wesleyan minister, Thomas Derrick, arrived on October 7, 1868, as the townsfolk began to rebuild after the fire. Within two weeks the church foundation had been laid. In a month it opened. The parishioners presented Reverend Derrick with a parsonage in October 1869 after his house washed away in a spring flood. The parsonage was moved to a safer location in 1874 and added to a house formerly occupied by Andrew Weldon, an Overlander of '62. In February 1914 the manse was leaning with a heavy load of snow, so it was pulled down. The church was torn down in the early 1900s. This building is a 1966 reconstruction based on photographs, with the addition of a belfry. The interior is sparsely furnished, as in the 1870s.

Rev. Thomas Derrick was a native of Cornwall, England, and had been a local preacher there for several years before coming to Canada in 1857. Leaving his Canada West circuits, he came to British Columbia, where he was a minister in Cariboo, Nanaimo, Victoria and New Westminster. Derrick had superior social qualities and was remarkably at ease with strangers. These attributes, combined with his excellent voice, fluent speaking style and remarkable memory, made him well suited for his work. His British Columbia travels hastened his failing health and in late 1879 he resigned to winter in California. In March 1880 he headed east by railway. A little east of Sacramento, on the Central Pacific Railway, "God took him." He is buried in Sacramento, California.

Rev. Thomas Derrick.
United Church of Canada

Williams Creek Christianity

While the Methodist Church and St. Saviour's are the physical evidence of Christianity on the creeks they were not the only missions to miners. In her book *Canada's Gold Rush Church*, Joan Weir details the efforts made toward miners.

Roman Catholics were first; in 1861 Father Grandidier held a service in Richfield. He was intimidated by what he viewed as immoral and profane miners. Also in 1861, Anglicans Rev. Luden Brown and Rev. Christopher Knipe held services in Antler Creek.

By 1862 Knipe had an irregular headquarters at Van Winkle; Rev. Sheepshanks was holding services at Antler; Rev. R.J. Dundas was visiting regularly, and Bishop George Hills made several visits.

None was particularly successful; all were appalled at the rough and rowdy miners who reserved Sundays for saloons, gambling, relaxation, drinking and fornication. When Brown made the mistake of speaking out against such behavior, not a single miner showed up for service.

Nevertheless, in 1863 Sheepshanks paid $500 for a lot in Richfield and built a small log church. Methodists Ephriam Evans and Arthur Browning did the same in Cameronton.

Weir says that as the mining community matured the men turned more toward church life, but at the same time the missionaries were short of funds and discouraged. In 1866 and 1867 not one service was held along the creek.

But in 1867 Welsh miners were granted a lot for the Cambrian Hall. Here they began weekly church services.

Organized religion really arrived in 1868 with Anglican Rev. James Reynard, who built St. Saviour's, Thomas Derrick at the Methodist Church and the Roman Catholics at St. Patrick's in Richfield.

Tommy Blair House   Lot 37

This house, now used for storage, was built for merchant Tommy Blair in 1933.

Miner's Boarding House/ Catlett House   Lot 38

This mid-1890s building was the home of Charles Catlett during the 1930s. According to Bill Hong, Catlett worked in the Cariboo Hospital until the early 1920s, also on the Waverly Hydraulic Mine and for the fisheries department at Bowron Lake. Catlett had a girlfriend who left him to marry a rival. A couple of years later Catlett disappeared. His clothing was found on the banks of the Fraser some time later.

The house is furnished as a boarding house for miners. In fact, boarding houses were quite different, although a home such as this might rent out a room to one or two miners. However, during Victorian times no self-respecting widowed or single women would rent rooms in their homes to men.

St. Saviour's Anglican Church   Lot 36

In Barkerville's early days, before 1885 and the relocation of the Cariboo Road through Devil's Canyon, St. Saviour's was the focal point of the bustling main street. One arrived from the south, from Richfield, and St. Saviour's stood as a beacon at the end of the road. It dominates early photos. When the road was relocated, the town's orientation changed. Chinatown was now at the end of town rather than the entrance, and St. Saviour's stood as a road block, not a focal point.

Rev. James Reynard acquired the lot for St. Saviour's Church in the spring of 1869 and began work in November. Before the Great Fire of 1868 he had held services in a saloon. The *Cariboo Sentinel* of November 21, 1868, described the church: "The new church building promises to be an elegant structure. It is being built from designs by the Rev. J. Reynard, which are being carried out by Messrs. Bruce and Mann. The style is early English. The church will consist of a nave, 30 by 20 feet and apsidal chancel 16 feet by 12 feet...A school room and vestry complete the building."

The man behind the church, Rev. Reynard, was 36 years old when he brought his wife and children to Barkerville in 1868. He had left his home in Hull, Yorkshire, two years previously and travelled to Vancouver Island as Indian missionary at Victoria and later the Principal of the Indian Mission. He was ordained when he volunteered to move to Barkerville. Reynard felt that "the church of England stands or falls in this effort."

There were many difficulties in building the church, for unlike the builders of the Methodist Church, Reynard received little help or encouragement from the miners. More popular were a series of Church Institute concerts he began—concerts still carried on today. Within a few years of arriving in Barkerville, Reynard's health was broken by the harsh climate, and in 1871 he moved to the coast. He died June 11, 1875, as Rector of St. Stephen's church in Saanich.

The architectural style of the Barkerville church is referred to as Gothic Revival, with the woodwork meant to suggest the stone Gothic churches of Europe that Reynard would have known in England. The siding is board and batten, commonly used in quick construction with green lumber. Green lumber would shrink and open cracks in the siding, but the covering battens shielded such cracks and lent a solid appearance in a country where most buildings were temporary. The decorative work and furnishings are thought to be crafted by Barkerville cabinetmaker John Endt. The church was formally opened September 18, 1870.

All the woodwork in St. Saviour's is original, as are the stove and most of the plain glass windows. The organ was donated in 1885 by Baroness Angela Burdett Coutts, a wealthy Englishwoman who was a friend of Bishop Hills, the first Bishop of British Columbia. The front porch was constructed in 1933, and the stained glass window was added in 1949 to honor the eightieth anniversary of the church. In 1970 the Masonic Lodge donated an electric air pump for the organ to replace the original leaking bellows. Until 1900 oil lamps were used for light, then gas lamps until 1934, when electric lights were installed. The church is owned and operated by the Diocese of Cariboo of the Anglican Church of Canada.

The Cariboo Wagon Road

Branching off the town's main street and curving along the west hillside perimeter of the parking lot and picnic grounds is an original stretch of the Cariboo Wagon Road—the road that connected Barkerville with the Royal Cariboo Hospital, the cemetery, Cameronton, Marysville and lower Williams Creek. Now closed to traffic, the road makes a fine walk for those wanting to visit the hospital site or the cemetery.

The road's location explains the orientation of the northernmost buildings in Barkerville, such as the Methodist Church, for they were built facing the main street—the Cariboo Road. The present lower road was pushed through during a wet spring when the hillside route was impassable. Since this road became more frequently used, it shifted the town's entrance.

Barkerville View Trail

As the creek valley became crowed, miners built cabins and even established claims on the hillsides. Early photos show that these buildings were accessed via a trail that ran along the hillside, which at times was clearcut. While this trail tended to shift over time, it offered a backdoor view of the town. In the late 1980s this trail was reopened by the Friends of Barkerville and Cariboo Goldfields Historical Society. It travels along the hillside to the upper part of Chinatown and is reached just a short distance north along the Cariboo Road from St. Saviour's church.

Cariboo Hospital

A few hundred feet north on the Cariboo Road is the site of the second Royal Cariboo Hospital. The history of the hospital and medical care is found under Gold Rush Society.

Dr. R.W.W. Carrall

A provincial "Stop Of Interest" sign near the Cariboo Hospital site gives a brief biography of Barkerville's Dr. R.W.W. Carrall.

"Of Ontario Loyalist stock, Carrall settled at Williams Creek in 1867, practising medicine and encouraging the depressed mining industry. He became the Cariboo representative on the colonial Legislative Council in 1868. On the 1870 Confederation delegation to Ottawa, he was the Canadian government's greatest ally. When British Columbia joined Canada in 1871, he was appointed one of the new province's first senators."

Cameronton Cemetery

One kilometre along the Cariboo Road, past the site of the Cariboo Hospital and the Shamrock mine of the 1930s, is the Cameronton Cemetery. Those buried there are listed in Appendix One.

This pre-fire main street scene shows many of the early businesses, including Nicolas Cunio's Brewery Saloon, the New England Bakery and Mundorf's Stable, later a dance hall. VPL #8637

Barkerville Jail

Where is the jail? A common question for visitors. The answer, in early years, was Richfield, which remained the centre of administration and government long after Barkerville matured. By 1870 Chartres Brew had bought a "gaol" building for $186, likely at this end of town. In 1875 the *Cariboo Sentinel* described it as a small but comfortable log building, one story, well mudded without, with double door and lined inside with planed lumber...two cells with the usual grating for the admission of air. No mattresses provided.

Historical interpreter Frank Cushman is Ned Stout, teamster, during the summer months on the creek.

The Valley of the Flags

On a windy day long ago, flags of almost every nation in the world fluttered and cracked on spruce poles hoisted high above the muddy main street of Barkerville. Each resident announced his nationality and patriotism with a banner. The flags of Prussia, the United States, Wales, Scotland, England, France, Germany, Canada and other countries gaily waved. Although it was at one time called Broadway by a few hopefuls, most residents thought of it, and newspapers wrote of it romantically, as the Valley of the Flags.

Main Street - The West Side

Williams Creek Schoolhouse Lot 34

The first mention of a teacher for Barkerville's growing population of children was in 1867, well after the hectic first years. Government representative H.M. Ball wrote Victoria that parents were willing to pay $2 per week to hire Mrs. Galloway as school mistress. The location was not recorded, but we know that the site bounced around town, from Stout's Gulch to the Masonic Hall.

This building was constructed in 1933 by Norman Scott and Red Swicker for James and Violet Doddy, who lived here until 1952. It was restored in 1977 to represent the schoolhouse.

William Bowron House Lot 32

Willie Bowron was born in Barkerville in 1872, the son of John and Emily Bowron. In 1898 he built this house, directly across the street from his parents, while working for various mining companies. Willie was a drinker, the black sheep of the family. A local sporting girl covered his debts, and when he moved to Bella Coola as telegraph operator she followed. They married and became respectable citizens.

The Willie Bowron house, like the Wendle house next door, represents a later period in Barkerville's development. During the first two decades there were few separate dwellings. Merchants lived behind or above their stores. The town was crowded, and there was no room for "unproductive" buildings in its core. Not until the late 1890s did this type of house come on the scene.

Wendle House Lot 31

The Wendle House was built in the 1890s by or for Alexander "Sandy" McArthur, a blacksmith. After changing hands several times, it was purchased by Joe Wendle and Beech LaSalle from the Fry family in 1904. When Wendle brought his wife Betty to Barkerville in about 1910, he bought out LaSalle's share.

Joe Wendle came from the U.S. He worked for several mining companies while developing prospects such as the Guyet, La Fontaine, Cunningham Creek claims and, with Beech LaSalle and John Bowron, the successful Hard-Up Claim on Grouse Creek.

Wendle and his wife established a Bowron Lake lodge and guiding business which operated until 1935. The Wendles also recognized the recreational potential of two small lakes (Bonner and Wendle) just north of Barkerville and eventually had them declared part of a park. To honor the couple's forethought, the Wendle name is preserved in Wendle Lake, Wendle Lake Provincial Park, and Betty Wendle Creek in Bowron Lake Provincial Park. In 1958, shortly before his death, Joe Wendle was presented a Certificate of Merit by the Lieutenant-Governor and the Premier of B.C. for his contributions to the Barkerville community.

This house had a porch at one time, likely added by the Wendles. The upstairs door is a feature of many buildings from this period. It provided access for large pieces of furniture and may also have been a fire escape. In the back was a garden tended by Betty Wendle.

Cameron & Ames Blacksmith Shop Lot 30

William Birnie Cameron, an owner of this shop, was born February 1839 in Lottingshire, Scotland. As a child he came with his parents to settle in Quebec, where he apprenticed to a blacksmith. He served four years at $25 a year plus board and lodging. When word of gold in Cariboo reached him, Cameron, then 23 years old, joined the Overlanders of '62 to cross from Canada. He financed the trip by borrowing $100. He received $90, ten percent being deducted as advance interest.

When Cameron reached Cariboo, he worked on the road before coming to Barkerville. His first money was sent east to repay the loan and pay off the mortgage on his father's farm. He went into business with James Amm (Ames) in 1869 as "Farriers and General

William B. Cameron.

PABC #52039

Blacksmiths." Cameron lived behind the shop in a small room with a bunk, stove and stool. He paid $25 a week for board at a place where one was expected to "walk in and eat as quickly as possible and leave room for someone else."

Cameron's story gives a view of the social life and structure of a gold rush town. In 1875 Samuel Greer sued him for "debauching his wife." Greer and his wife were both from Canada West via California. They had been running a saloon on Jack of Clubs Creek, but Greer went south to farm land near Chilliwack in 1872. Some folks thought he had abandoned his wife, but when he came back and found "Cameron lying on my bed" he shouted he would "murder you the first chance I get."

Wellington Moses, who kept a regular journal of town events, testified that he had seen Mrs. Greer "leaving Cameron's house at all hours between 10 at night and 5 in the morning."

However, Greer could not convince his peers that he was the wronged party and that Cameron "had made a whore of my wife." The jury found for Cameron.

Irish Sam Greer moved to his Chilliwack farm, then to land near the growing city of Vancouver. Here he battled the CPR, who took his waterfront land. Greer got two years in the penitentiary for obstruction. His beach was named Kitsilano, not Greer's.

The greater part of 1870s blacksmithing involved shoeing express horses and mules and making tools for the mining trade. Iron was packed in 500 miles; shoes and nails were made by hand. Charcoal was produced by local charcoal burners, such as Greenbury Harris.

Amm left in 1872, but Cameron carried on pounding an anvil until October 1875, when he sold the business to C.P. O'Neill and returned east for a family visit. There he met and married Elizabeth

Margaret Gardiner, a school teacher, settled near Dewittville, Quebec, and raised a family of three boys and five girls. Cameron died in Huntingdon, Quebec, January 28, 1919.

American blacksmith Charles Patrick O'Neill opened here in 1875, married 16-year-old Maryanne in 1878 and raised two children, Martha Washington and William John, known as Mattie and Wiggs. O'Neill was killed in the winter of 1886-87 while shoeing one of Barnard's Express horses. It kicked him across the shop and drove him into a pointed stick. He died that night.

The blacksmith shop stood until the 1930s when it was torn down and replaced with this garage, now displaying a wheelwright's and blacksmithing shop.

F.J. Barnard's Express Lot 28

Francis J. Barnard started his express company in 1861 by carrying letters to the gold creeks on foot. Within a few years he was operating the longest stagecoach run in North America, Yale to Barkerville. The building was begun in May 1869, according to the diary of black barber Moses. By August the company's name was being lettered and the workers had moved in. Ten years later it was rented to the San Francisco Quartz Mining Company.

During stagecoach days, which only ended about 1914, the express office was the hub of the town's activity. Stages brought in long awaited mail, friends, children from school, visitors, new dance hall girls, merchant and madams. Freight and goods kept the town alive, and it all passed through these doors. The boardwalk was piled high with goods, the walls plastered with bills and schedules, the air filled with stories and rumors of the towns and people down the line.

This structure was constructed in 1968, based on 1869 photographs. No longer a stage depot, it serves as the ticket office for the Theatre Royal.

Goldfields Bakery Lot 27

Early morning visitors to Barkerville are often greeted by the mouth-watering aroma of freshly baked sourdough, scones and bannock. The odors come from this shop, the Goldfields Bakery. This building was constructed in 1933 as the Red Front Cigar Store and Buckley's Drug Store—thus the two front doors—with living quarters upstairs. In 1969 the building was renovated to house the bakery, based on a bakery here in the 1930s.

The Post Office Lot 26

The Barkerville Post Office, operating during summer months, is a 1964 reconstruction based on photographs, of an 1869 building on this site that housed the Bank of British North America. By 1879 the building was used as a postal and telegraph office. It burned down on May 18, 1946. It is considered to be the eighth oldest continually operating post office in the province. The tall doors are a matter of style, designed to let light in, rather than a response to tall miners or deep snows, as has been suggested by some.

The first postage stamps were issued in 1861, from "British Columbia and Vancouver Island." They bore a profile of Queen Victoria on a pink background and were printed in twopence and halfpenny values. Decimal currency came into use in 1862, so two new stamps of five- and ten-cent value were introduced in 1865.

Early gold rush communication was limited to word of mouth and mail. The importance of the mail cannot be overestimated. Letters from the east often took months, during which time people had died, children had been born and mortgages foreclosed. There is the story, for instance, of the miner who after several years of labor sent his wife a letter and the fare west, asking her to bring herself and their small child to join him. She left, but by the time she arrived her husband had died in a mill accident. True to the code of the day, his friends made sure she and the child were cared for.

Other examples of the importance and peculiarity of 1800s mail service are the personal letters of Robert Harkness. Harkness was an Overlander, a storekeeper with a wife and three children (one of just two weeks) when he headed west. Travellers heading into the wilderness of the west wrote at every opportunity as they approached the frontier, always hoping for that one last letter from home. At Detroit Harkness wrote:

I was sure the one I wrote from Toronto had got home and that I should have an answer here this morning, at the latest. The first thing I did when I got up this morning was to strike a beeline for the post-office and when I found nothing I was awfully disappointed. I am more homesick than ever I was in my life before but if I had a letter from you it would half cure me.

Prairie travellers often had to rely on someone eastbound to carry mail and forward it at the next town. One method, called "making up a mail," involved tying letters in a waterproof packet and leaving them in a conspicuous place at a campsite or along the trail, with a request that travellers bound in the opposite direction should carry and pass on the mail. This was, to say the least, unreliable. At one point on his way west Harkness wrote, "*It is almost three months since your last letter to me was written & what may not have occurred since that? How sincerely I pray that you may all be well.*"

When travelers reached the "civilization" of the goldfields or the coastal towns there were still frustrations, for mail could be obtained only at the end of day-long lineups. Unemployed miners would sell their places in line to the more affluent. But the wait or the payment to avoid a wait might still be made in vain.

Robert Harkness reached Williams Creek in 1863 and wrote a series of melancholy letters to his wife Sabrina, always mentioning how he missed her and their children, how he hoped to be home soon, how he always thought of her, and what life was like on the creek. In June 1863 he wrote:

I suppose you will be longing to hear from me before this reaches you but I have not been able to write to you sooner. ...Provisions are high here. Pack animals can come no farther than Van Winkle...everything coming here from there has to be carried on men's backs for which they get 25 cents a pound. I did a little of it but it is very severe labor. ...You must pardon my writing on such a dirty sheet of paper but it cost me a quarter & I was too stingy to throw it away because it got soiled. It will cost me another quarter for an envelope & two dollars to send the letter to New Westminster. ...I had hoped that the express that came in here yesterday would have brought me a letter but it didn't. ...

A year later, Harkness wrote from New Westminster: *I got a letter from you the other day dated March 1863 & addressed "Bob Harkness" so it was about two years in reaching me. The Postmaster had the impudence to tell me he was burning up some old newspapers & found that little letter in one and said I had better tell my folks not to enclose letters in newspapers. Well, even if he does steal some of my papers you must still continue sending as a newspaper is the next best thing to a letter.*

Robert Harkness stayed in Cariboo for four years, and like many miners returned home no wealthier than he left.

The Cariboo Gold Escort prepares to leave Barkerville in 1863. Charles Gentile photo. PABC #8941

J.P. Taylor's Drug Store Lot 25

In 1866 James Taylor opened Barkerville's first drug store, with a wide variety of drugs and patent medicines, newspapers and cigars. This store burned down in the 1868 fire, but as the ashes cooled, Taylor and David Lewis were rebuilding. Taylor operated his drug store on one side, and Lewis operated a barber shop, dentist office and bath house on the other. Lewis advertised that he was "prepared to fill teeth with gold, silver or tin foil, set teeth on pivots, repair plates and extract teeth."

In May 1873 a notice appeared in the *Cariboo Sentinel: David Lewis, an old and good colored citizen, died Tuesday at his Barkerville residence. Barber for a number of years. Native of Columbus Ohio. Age 60.*

The building's subsequent history is unknown. Reconstruction is based on similar buildings. Future renovations may see this made into two separate businesses again.

Barkerville Brewery and Brewery Hotel Lot 24

The empty lot between the drug store and the Masonic Hall held a series of buildings. The first was the Barkerville Brewery and the Brewery Hotel, built before the fire and rebuilt afterwards. The hotel was a large building with 14 rooms. The Brewery's Triple X Ale won several prizes in the 1870 fairs. Its quality may have been the result of natural spring water drawn from the hill behind. In the late 1870s owner Nicolas Cunio, an Italian who came to the creek in the early 1860s, sold the brewery for about $3000 and then a couple of years later brought it back for $1000. It appears he was one of the few people who could make it work. The building burned down in the 1880s.

The empty lots also held a Chinese store, later Fanny Bendixon's Boarding House, and in the late 1880s an outdoor ice-skating rink. It had a snowshed roof and walls of banked snow, illuminated at night by torch lights.   ✦

Masonic Hall Lot 23

As soon as men arrived on Williams Creek, Masonic brethren began meeting in the coffee houses and reading rooms of Barkerville and Cameronton. When the *Cariboo Sentinel* began, the editor encouraged "the brethren on the creeks" that the celebration of St. John's day, a date important to Masonry, should not be omitted. By October 1866 there were regular weekly meetings, and two months later Jonathan Nutt took papers to Victoria from the 14 Cariboo Masons asking for endorsement as a lodge. He returned in April 1867 with a dispensation for Cariboo Lodge No. 469. As many men were from the California goldfields, they adopted the "California rituals" of masonry.

The inaugural meeting was held June 24, 1868, with a feast of St. John in the evening. That afternoon the 27 members climbed the hill to the new cabin of Jonathan Nutt and had their photograph taken, resplendent in aprons and sashes.

When "The Most Worshipful Grand Lodge of Ancient, Free and Accepted Masons of British Columbia" was formed in 1871, the lodge was given the designation No. 4 BCR. By this time the membership was about 50, though it declined with the fortunes of Barkerville.

Soon after becoming official, and immediately after the fire of 1868, the Masons arranged with "Messrs. Bruce and Mann to build a commodious hall over the new building they are erecting on the lot formerly occupied [before the fire] by the Occidental Hotel."

In February 1869 the *Sentinel* reported "The Bank of B.C. will be removed to Bruce and Mann's new building on March 10th, the upper story of which is now occupied by Cariboo Lodge #469 F&AM as their lodge room."

This Bruce and Mann building, which later served as a schoolhouse as well, burned in 1937. The next year a new hall was constructed, and in 1967 a facade resembling the original 1869 buildings was added.

Joe Denny's Saloon Lot 22

The saloons of Barkerville ranged from large, noisy dance halls to small, friendly rooms like Joe Denny's. The original building on which this reconstruction is based was first a tailor shop operated by Colin McCallum, an Overlander of '62. McCallum rebuilt after the fire and then sold to Perrett and Harding in 1870, who operated the unlikely combination of a tailor shop and saloon.

Joe Denny was here by 1863 and was active in all facets of the community, though he was particularly known as Captain of the fire brigade. He operated this saloon from May 1879 until his death in September 1891.

The House Hotel Lot 21

The original House Hotel building was constructed in 1869 as a general store run by Angelo Pendola, an Italian merchant. In the 1870s it became home for "The Mechanics Institute," later the library and then the telegraph office. In 1884 it was purchased by Charlie and Margaret House as a hotel. The hotel reconstruction now represents a saloon. It flies the American flag as an indication of Charlie House's strong American patriotism.

Charlie House of Syracuse, New York, arrived in Williams Creek in the late 1860s and went to work at a claim on Conklin Gulch, and later on Jack of Clubs Creek. House was popular, handsome, witty, respected and liked by miners and their families alike. When John and Jeanette Houser returned to the creeks in 1875, they brought with them Mrs. Houser's younger sister Margaret. Margaret Houser and Charlie House were married the next summer.

The House Hotel, now an operating restaurant.

85

In 1885 the Houses established the House Hotel, soon to be a favorite stopping place for miners who appreciated the home-like atmosphere. The House Hotel was more of a boarding house, with people taking rooms for long periods. After Charlie died in 1913 Margaret continued to run the hotel until 1939. Charlie and Margaret had two children, Joe and Wesley Charles. The Houses are both buried in the Barkerville cemetery.

McPherson's Watchmaker's Shop

This replica building depicts what the newspaper described as "a handsome little building" erected by A.D McPherson in November 1868, immediately after the fire. For two years it was used by the Bank of British North America, but in June 1869 McPherson moved his business here. The business was short lived as he died in July 1870.

The building was then used as a boot and shoe store by C.A. Noltmeyer and later a house for the Norburg brothers. See both in the Cameronton Cemetery section.

Mason & Daly General Store & C. Strouss Merchants Lot 20 C & B

These two buildings have undergone many changes. The one on the right was originally the Hudson's Bay Company Store, built in 1868 by Messrs. Bruce and Mann. It had an office and bedroom attached and a fire and frost-proof stone warehouse between the two buildings. The warehouse disappears from photos in the 1880s, when the store (on the right) was moved closer.

The Strouss store was built in 1868 and had lean-to living quarters. It was sold to Charles Oppenheimer in 1871, a year later to F. Neufelder. In 1880 the HBC bought the store. In 1885 Mason and Daly took over both buildings. The buildings were in good shape in the 1940s. However, volunteer fire departments could earn $100 for equipment by burning down potential fire hazards. The 1868 stores were torched to earn the Wells Fire Department $200. The present buildings are a reconstruction based on photographs.

Prior to their Mason and Daly store, Joe Mason and John Daly operated the Antelope Restaurant and saloon. Mason had an interest in the Heron claim, brought in cattle and operated a dairy farm in Pleasant Valley three miles north. The dairy buildings can still be seen a short distance east on the 3100 Road. Joe Mason died in 1890 and is buried in the Cameronton cemetery.

Van Volkenburgh Cabin Lot 19

Originally called the Nason House for a family that lived here in the 1930s, this building is an example of Cariboo Add-on Architecture. It was thought this was a 1900s dwelling until a one-room log cabin was discovered beneath the walls. The cabin, since dated to about 1870, was built by or for Benjamin Van Volkenburgh, butcher and cattle dealer. He married Anne Cameron, a divorcee with three children, in April 1869. It is thought they lived here until 1874. In 1880 T. Harding took it over. Later Senator S.A. Rogers owned the house. When Rogers died, Floyd DeWitt Reed, an American trapper and guide in the Bowron country, moved in. In 1933 E.J. Avison bought it and sold to Oliver Nason. (See the Nason story in Gold Rush Society.)

This succession is typical of Barkerville buildings. The log cabin became a bungalow with a bay window. It has been returned to its 1870s facade, with 1890 and 1910 additions on the back.

Cariboo Sentinel Print Shop Lot 18

The first *Cariboo Sentinel* came off the press June 17, 1865, in "Barkerville, Williams Creek, British Columbia," a four-page weekly paper, edited and owned by George Wallace and sold for $1 a copy.

Under various owners the *Cariboo Sentinel* was printed until 1875. (See Gold Rush Society.) Copies of all editions exist today, a valuable record for a decade of Barkerville's life. After the Great Fire of 1868 the *Sentinel* moved to the Louie Blanc Photo Studio building at this location. The building was torn down before 1900. As no photographs or descriptions exist, this 1967 construction is based on speculation. The office houses an operating print shop using period presses.

Dr. Callanan's/Mrs. Neate's House Lot 17

This house was built in the 1890s for Dr. Callanan, an Irish physician at the Cariboo Hospital, and restored in 1965. (From 1909 to 1916 Callanan was the Conservative representative for Cariboo in the Legislative Assembly.) This log building is covered on three sides with drop siding to lend a more finished appearance. Since Dr. Callanan was not a Barkerville resident in 1870, the house represents the dressmaking establishment of Mrs. Neate, listed in the 1871 British Columbia Directory as a Barkerville dressmaker.

Maria Neate was 20 years old, a widow with a two-year-old child when she came to Barkerville. She married George Byrnes, who ran the Boomerang Bowling Alley, in November 1874. She used her legal name, Halley. Mrs. Neate may have been a "grass widow," a divorcee; or perhaps she was a widow of convenience, that is, a woman with a child born out of wedlock. When Mary Pinkerton died in 1880, Maria took her and John Pinkerton's children in.

It should also be noted, though not to cast any aspersions on the present resident, that the term dressmaker was a common Victorian euphemism for prostitute, so much so that only the context of the word would define the woman's occupation.

Kerr Brewery Lot 16

Little information exists about the James H. Kerr and Son Phoenix Brewery, except that it appears in a September 1869 photograph and was mentioned in the July issue of the *Cariboo Sentinel*. Kerr brewed Columbia Pale Ale and Porter, not the usual lager. Perhaps the competition with Cunio's Barkerville Brewery down the road was too stiff, for in 1871 he closed and offered the building for sale or rent. The name Phoenix and the image of a creature rising from its own ashes were popular with businesses that rebuilt after the fire.

The 1980 reconstruction houses toilets and a rest area.

Carpenter Shop Lot 16a

This building was originally a lean-to attached to the Kwong Lee Butcher Shop. It illustrates a small 1880s carpentry shop, though Johnny Knott would not have used this facility. The best example of his work is the ornate Barkerville Hotel—built in 1869 and one of the few original buildings still standing. Johnny Knott (a perfect name for a carpenter) was also the headboard and coffin maker.

Chinatown

Kwong Lee Wing Kee Co. Manager's Residence Lot 16

This residence for the manager of a large Chinese company was built in 1901 by Tsant How Quon and is all that remains of the company buildings. The story has it that the manager ordered a large fence built around the dwelling, a Chinese custom to protect his wife from prying eyes. The company the manager controlled—Kwong Lee Company, predecessor to the Kwong Lee Wing Kee Company—was one of the largest and most complex businesses in Barkerville. The company was established in Victoria and New Westminster as early as February 1860 and followed the gold rush north. By 1864 they operated a branch at Quesnel and an advertisement in the *Cariboo Sentinel's* first edition of June 6, 1865, suggests an established Cariboo firm.

The Kwong Lee Company's Barkerville store was open by June 1866 on property that Celine Armand sold to two brothers, Loo Chuck Fan and Loo Choo Fan, principal partners in the company. The sale involved land plus "a dwelling house, a small building attached to said premises, tenements and appurtenances."

Tsang Quan, Chinese Merchant. This photograph was taken in the Qwong Lee Wing Kee manager's residence in the early 1900s. BVHP #Q0531

As a retail and wholesale general merchandiser, the Kwong Lee Company advertised, "a Large Stock of Groceries, Provisions, Rice, Tea, Sugar, Cigars, Tobacco, Opium, Clothing, Boots and Shoes, Hardware and Mining Tools which are offered for sale at Reasonable Rates." The store operated in connection with firms in San Francisco, Canton and

Hong Kong. By 1868 there were branches in Yale, Lillooet, Quesnelle Forks, Quesnel and Barkerville. It could be said that the Kwong Lee Company ran the first chain store in British Columbia.

In the 1868 fire all buildings and stock were destroyed. The company's loss was appraised at $40,000, the third largest of any individual or company in Barkerville. After the fire the company immediately rebuilt in the same location and began to branch out, buying more land, investing in the Cariboo Gold Quartz venture and, by the 1880s, acting as a banker for residents.

Like the rest of Barkerville, the Kwong Lee holdings dwindled in the 1880s. By 1885 a receiver had been appointed for the troubled company and in 1888 Gee Wing was indicated as the assignee or purchaser of the Kwong Lee Estate. His firm was known as the Kwong Lee Wing Kee Company and operated until after 1900.

The manager's residence represents the once prosperous Chinese firm and the residence of a Chinese businessman who enjoyed a far more affluent lifestyle than the common Chinese miner.

Cabin Lot 15

This post-1900 dwelling is now used for storage.

The empty lots between lots 14 and 15 were once occupied by the Wah Lee and Kwong Lee wood yards.

Callanan Garage Lot 14C

This garage, of a late period, may have been used by Dr. Callanan.

Kibbee House and original New England Bakery Lot 14B

In Barkerville's later years the distinct boundaries of Chinatown faded, and many homes for non-Chinese were found in Chinatown. The Kibbee House is an example. The house also exemplifies the research that continues and the discoveries still being made in Barkerville. The house is named for the Kibbee family who lived here in 1918 and who figure in the history of the Bowron Lake country, where Frank Kibbee was a guide and lodge owner.

However, the original building was constructed about 1869 and was located down the street between Louie Blanc photo studio, which may have been part of the building, and Dr. Jones' office, as Fick's New England Bakery and Coffee Saloon. About 1917 Kibbee moved the building here, where a few windows and some rear rooms were added. Beneath the exterior siding is the original work, still in good shape, and beneath the interior wallboard lies the old wallpaper. When the time comes for restoration work, this house will provide researchers with interesting material. Unfortunately, some of the additions have had to be removed due to rot.

Water Lines

Overhead water lines are an example of early waterworks. Small diameter trees were cut down and laboriously sawn in half, then hollowed out and bound together to form a pipe. The hillside above the town has many springs, and it was then, as now, a good source of domestic water. At one time there was a suggestion that the town be named Springfield in keeping with Richfield and because of the numerous hillside springs. Springs were especially important because the creek was usually a muddy stream where men and machinery sloshed around and fouled the waters.

Wa Lee Store Lot 14A

This display represents a typical Chinese general store catering to both Orientals and Caucasians. On the shelves are rice, samsui (rice wine) in small jugs with a tiny neck, porcelain dishes, Chinese baskets and opium, which in the mining days was legal and popular with both Chinese and Caucasians. The small fiddle-shaped wooden cases hanging on the wall contain a portable gold scale of brass and ivory.

The Chinese known as Wa Lee, who ran this store, was established in Barkerville soon after the first miner had dirty clothes to wash. In a pre-fire photograph we see "Wa Lee Washing and Ironing" at the north end of the street, one of several Chinese businesses located in the main section of town.

Wa Lee was one of those Chinese who were accepted in the white community. Wiggs O'Neill remarked in 1880 that "when there would be a big do or party everyone would be there, even to Moses the colored barber and Wah Lee, the big Tyee Chinaman merchant."

Wa Lee may not have been the proper name of the man. Chinese often named their businesses after a favorite phrase or a line of poetry. Wa Lee, for instance, might translate as "Peace and Harmony" or "Righteousness and Goodness." The proprietor then became known by his business's name.

Whatever his name, when fire destroyed Wa Lee's original building, he built a small wash house, which he operated until 1875. At that time he followed many Barkerville merchants and moved to Lightning Creek in response to the new activity. By the time he returned in 1882, his business had changed; Wa Lee's was no longer simply a wash house. He had taken partners and obtained licences for liquor, retail goods and opium—all more profitable than laundry. Eventually a larger store was built on the lot next door, near the wood lot. Each month a partner would drive pigs from Quesnel to Barkerville, where they were slaughtered and delivered to the surrounding mining camps.

When Wa Lee left Barkerville in 1907, his two stores were taken over by a group of five Chinese known as the Sing Kee Company. Both buildings were destroyed by fire in 1914. This building was moved from Wells in 1973 and restored to resemble Wa Lee's store.

Yan War Store Lot 13

This display reflects a store of the 1870s, with open bins of food of interest to Chinese and Caucasians.

During building restoration many interesting artifacts are found. In the case of the Yan War Store, newspapers dating to 1873 were found beneath the upstairs floorboards, indicating that it is one of Barkerville's oldest structures. Evidence suggests the lower floor was built sometime before 1873 and the upper storey added around 1874. During reconstruction five layers of floorboards were uncovered, each one showing a different wear pattern and suggesting a different use. The main floor walls show signs of extensive shelving, indicating that the earliest occupants used it as a store. At the turn of the century it was known as the Yan War Store.

Garage Lot 12

This simple structure shows how mining town buildings changed use and how difficult it is to ascertain when and why buildings were erected. A Sam Toy came to Barkerville about 1909 and worked as a partner in the Lun Wo Company. He lived in a building on this lot. Another report says that Tan You Company occupied the cabin at some time. As the building now resembles a garage, it is difficult to know if this is the original structure lived in by Sam Toy, having been made more utilitarian, or whether the original was torn down and replaced with this garage.

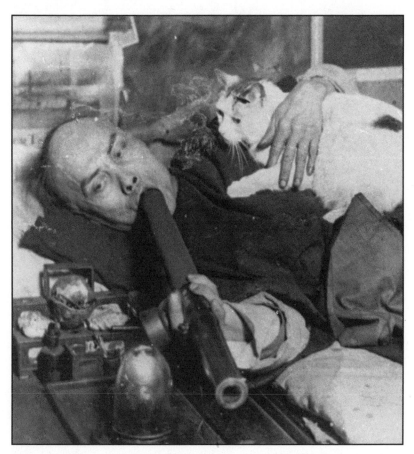

Opium smoking was a popular escape for many Chinese and some Caucasians. Its use was legal until 1908. San Francisco Archives

Min Yee Tong Lot 10

Chinese tongs have, for the most part, been misunderstood by western society. They are seen as secret criminal associations, like the Mafia. Although some were, tongs generally were fraternal associations

91

The Wa Lee Store interior.

based on clan, surname or locality. The word tong (*t'ang*) translated literally means "hall," as in a meeting hall. The tongs or fraternities played a major role in North American Chinese communities, particularly a mining camp, where men were cut off from friends and family. The tongs served as boarding houses, hospitals, old-age homes, gambling halls and community centers. In a broader context, they served as political organizations dedicated to protecting Chinese rights and preserving Chinese language and culture.

One aspect of Chinese culture was gambling, represented on the rear wall of this tong house by the "White Dove" lottery. This was a version of the numbers racket involving 88 numbers. Draws were made several times a day. Chinese "runners" circulated up and down the boardwalks and back streets of Barkerville collecting bets and then later distributed winnings. Profits helped keep the tong operating. In some gambling houses, walls were painted white because it was the color of the spirit world and therefore unlucky for the gamblers and profitable for the house.

The posters are originals discovered under wallpaper during restoration. Also posted are the rules of mahjong, another gambling game depicted here. Fantan was played with beads and a bowl and involved guessing whether an even or odd number would come up.

Fantan beads are found in the floor cracks and the foundations of many Chinese buildings.

According to the Min Yee Tong, they have owned the tong house since before 1894. The weathering of the siding, the square nails and the wear patterns throughout indicate that the tong house may date to the time of the Great Fire or before.

Kwong Sang Wing Store Lot 7

The Kwong Sang Wing Company constructed this building in the late 1890s, according to most accounts—although archaeological work in 1980 indicates the site may have been occupied much earlier. Restoration work involved complete dismantling and rebuilding, replacing rotted logs and rebuilding the porch and lean-to.

The main floor was a general store and the upper floor a residence for proprietor Eng Fong, his wife and four children. The family returned to China in 1915, but the store continued to operate for many years. The Kwong Sang Wing Company was an important business in turn-of-the-century Barkerville and owned several lots and buildings.

The building is now an operating Chinese general store.

Terrace Gardens

Chinese miners no sooner started mining the bars of the Fraser, Thompson and Quesnel Rivers than they used what little extra time they had to plant gardens. All along the rivers they rented or squatted on garden plots, often bordering mining claims, where they grew vegetables and fruit to supplement their diet. If they had extra they sold it. As the land was steep and water precious, they utilized a terrace system as they had in Kwung Tung province. Considerable research has been done on similar sites in Idaho and it is known that there are many similar Chinese gardens in B.C.

On the hillside above and behind the empty lots south of the Kwong Sang Wing Store is the rock work of terrace gardens the Chinese built along Williams Creek. Though the growing season at this elevation of 4500 feet is short, the terraces served to trap warm air and delay frosts on chilly nights. There is no record and no sign of what was grown here, but the crops grown in Idaho varied from root crops to rhubarb, strawberries and grapes. In the *Cariboo Sentinel* there is mention of the Chinese taking over the fresh vegetable market, so these gardens, or similar ones, must have been successful.

Diller Corridor

This end of town is sometimes referred to as the Diller Corridor for the Diller claim a short distance north. The story of I.P. Diller is told in the Gold Rush Society section.

The Bulkhead

The bulkhead or creekside dam built in 1872 to contain the creek keeps the water of the creek much further away than in 1872. At that time the road was squeezed against the hillside, as seen in early photos.

This is the beginning of the Last Mile walk to Richfield Court House, two kilometres south.

Main Street - The East Side

The walking tour now goes down the east side of Main Street to St. Saviour's church.

Chinese Miner's Cabin Lot 78
This late 1880s cabin depicts the living arrangements of Chinese miners. Meals were often eaten at the tong house, so the stove would only have been used for heating. The blankets are a Chinese design and the poster typical of those seen in Chinese buildings.

Mrs. Houser's House Lot 77
Jeanette Houser (nee Ceise) came from Germany to Barkerville in 1867, probably as a Hurdy Gurdy girl. After the Great Fire she left, either to return to Germany or for San Francisco. In San Francisco in 1870 she married John Houser, a Barkerville miner who was wintering in California. She may have met Houser on the creeks years before.

In 1871 the Houser family, now including young son William, came to Barkerville, but stayed only a year before returning to San Francisco. In 1875 the Housers were drawn back to Barkerville again, this time accompanied by three children and Houser's sister Margaret. Margaret later married Charlie House of the House Hotel.

During their years in Barkerville John Houser worked at his claims—the San Juan was one—and he and Jeanette took an active part in community life. Of particular interest to them was the Dramatic Society. John was an accomplished musician and a popular violinist, in demand for dances and parties along the creek. He taught each child to play an instrument and soon had a Houser orchestra.

As the boys grew they joined the crew at the Houser claim, where a cave-in collapsed on 19-year-old Billy Houser, forcing amputation of one leg. John Houser died in the spring of 1900, but the boys kept prospecting and digging. One of the claims was the Ketch Mine, a hydraulic operation opened in 1921 by Billy Houser and John MacDougall, where in 1937 a 16-ounce nugget surfaced.

Jeanette Houser outlived her husband by many years. She stayed in Barkerville and greeted visitors with stories of the old days. Not all visitors were polite. Some insisted on taking photographs, barged through her home and sometimes almost took possession. In later years Jeanette Houser considered this location "out of the town center." She once remarked that she "had to go down-town to the stores once a month" but hadn't got to it yet this month. In 1933 this grand old lady of Barkerville was found dead on the floor by her nephew Joe House.

This display depicts the residence as it was when Jeanette Houser lived here. The house's age is unknown, but during restoration in 1980 and 1983 newspapers dating from 1897 were found pasted on the wall.

Barker Company Shaft Lot 75C
The Barker Company had eight partners, each with a claim of 100 feet—so the entire claim ran 800 feet down the creek from this point to the vicinity of the Theatre Royal where a second shaft, the actual discovery shaft, was sunk. Although it was more usual to start at a claim's lower end and work upstream, thereby having less drainage

trouble, the Barker Company men knew where the lead, the gold vein, was on other claims and did not want to drift or tunnel too far away. They decided to deal with water here and follow the lead downstream.

Over a period of several years, the Barker Company claim took out $600,000 in gold. In the 1860s a full one-eighth share was valued at between $10,000 and $20,000. Barker's story is told in the Gold Rush Society section.

Shafts and tunnels such as those of the Barker Company undermined the streets and buildings of Barkerville, and their frequent collapse caused more than a few problems. In 1871 a Barker Company shaft collapsed beneath P. Manetta's Miners' Provision Store.

This street arch in Chinatown celebrated a visiting dignitary. W.D. Moses may be the third man from the left. L.A. Blanc photo. PAC #C61937

Sing Kee Herbalist Lot 75B

The Chinese medicine practised by Sing Kee traces its origins and development through thousands of years. It is based on the healing powers of herbs, minerals and animal products. Those who practised this medicine were known as herbalists, though herbs played only a small part in the practitioner's knowledge and cures. Herbalists were found in most Chinese communities in gold rush British Columbia.

Sing Kee purchased imported medicines for this shop from China, by way of Victoria and San Francisco, and gathered native plants such as chamomile or sage. He may also have grown some of his own herbs in the terraced gardens across the road, but as the strength of the medicines was attributed to the region where they grew, it is more likely they came from China.

This cabin, an example of crude log dovetailing, houses the shop of herbalist Sing Kee as it would have appeared in 1870. The building's origin is questionable. In appearance, the Sing Kee Store and the Gee Quon House belong to the immediate post-fire era, but they do not show up in early photos. It is thought this building dates from 1868.

Gee Quon Residence Lot 75
This residence was built between 1885 and 1900.

Lee Chong's Store   Lot 73
This two-storey 1930s building was a general store operated by Bill Hong, a resident of the 1900s whose company was known as the Lee Chong Company. It is another good example of Cariboo Add-on Architecture: Hong kept extending the building backward to solve his storage problems. In recent years the rear additions have been torn down as unsalvagable.

(There is an entrance to Barkerville's back street at this point, described later in this guide.)

Chih Kung T'ang Lot 69B
The Chih Kung T'ang, earlier known as the Hung Shun T'ang, was a North American expression of the Triad Society, an association that traces its origins far back into Chinese history. In 1644 the Mongolian hordes of Manchuria swept down from the north and overthrew the Ming dynasty of the Chinese Empire. "Triads" or secret societies were formed to restore the Ming dynasty, the name based on the myth of the three knights who founded the order. The Triad motto was, "Overthrow darkness, restore the light," a thinly veiled reference to the light of the Ming dynasty. One name the Triad Society was known by translates as the "Patriotic Rising Society."

The T'ang came to North America during the California gold rush then traveled north with the Chinese who sought gold in British Columbia. This Barkerville lodge, established by Skenkui Huang in 1863, was Canada's first. As well as secretly supporting the Chinese government's overthrow, it offered social, cultural and political contact for over 1000 Cariboo Chinese who where strangers in a strange land, in much the same way as the Welsh Cambrian Society or the Freemason's did for Caucasian miners. The T'ang went a step further. According to Dr. David Lai, "it controlled the socio-economic activities of most miners not only in Barkerville but also in other parts of the Cariboo." As well as being a fraternal and political society it acted as a welfare organization and a court for settling disputes amongst members. It wielded a powerful influence over all Chinese residents.

In 1882/83 the Hung Shun T'ang, under master Nuanta Chen, changed their name to the Chih Kung T'ang. The next masters were Wofeng Ho, 1888-1890; Wong Hung, Dea Wai Suey and Chong Quin, 1890-1917 and Dea Song, 1917-1950.

When the Manchu dynasty was overthrown by Sun Yat Sen in 1912, it was with the financial support of the Chih Kung T'angs throughout China and North America. With the T'ang's raison d'être gone, a change in name was in order, so it became the Chih Kung Party. In 1946 the Hung Leaque Congress decided to change all their societies to "The Chinese Freemasons Party." As the Barkerville T'ang

The Chih Kung T'ang building, seen here before being moved for archeological purposes.

was declining there is no evidence that they followed suit.

The Chih Kung T'ang had three buildings, this general hostel and gathering place, a hospital such as the cabin next door, and a meeting hall down the street near the Lung Duck Tong with various levels of rooms and altars for use by members of different status in the organization.

Some restoration work has been done on the roof and porch in recent years. In 1992 the building was moved off its foundation to allow a 1993 archeological dig. Hopefully the results will explain not only the history of the building but something of the people who lived here.

The red sign above the door reads: "The Branch of Chinese the Hung Leaque Chih Kung Party," reflecting the 1945 name change. The two blue posters contain classical couplets. The characters on the left translate as, "Outside nine mountains lie beautifully verdant." The characters on the right say, "Inside the temple three gods are solemnly seated." The three gods would be Lao Tzu, Buddha and Confucius.

Tai Ping Fong Lot 69A

The Tai Ping Fong or Peace Room was an old-age home and a hospital, a place where Chinese could spend their final days in comfort. It was always the intention of Chinese to return to their homeland when they earned enought money to ensure a comfortable life but, as with their Caucasian brother miners, this goal often eluded them. Poverty, sickness or age might make the final pilgrimage impossible. In these cases, it was up to the Chinese community,

97

usually the tongs, to become responsible for those stranded in a foreign land. It is not certain that this building was, in fact, the building used as a hospital.

Dannhauer/Halverson House Lot 69

This house was constructed in 1939 by Vince and Gunner Halverson. Originally this area was part of Chinatown but plans include making this building into a mining display.

Nam Sing, the earliest Chinese man in Cariboo, arrived about 1860. He grew vegetables near Quesnellemouth and freighted produce and hay to Barkerville. PABC #HP68805

Lung Duck Tong Restaurant Lot 66

The Lung Duck Tong was another Chinese fraternal organization. This 1970s reconstruction is being more freely interpreted as a tea house or restaurant. A tea room was a common feature of community life in southern China. Men could come here and spend a few hours in conversation with friends while being offered a snack or lunch, *Dim Sum,* small dough-wrapped delicacies stuffed with seafood, meat, mushrooms, chestnuts or any number of other tasty morsels. This building is now an operating restaurant where visitors can sample similar food.

Sporting House Lot 65

Both this building, representing a small "sporting house" or brothel and the term itself, are anachronisms, for neither came into use until the 1930s. In the 1870s a Chinese named Ah Mow ran a brothel near this spot. Ah Mow was here as early as 1866. Among other things, Ah Mow was a pimp, an occupation that led to his death.

In the summer of 1871 he "turned out" John Baker, alias Jean Boulanger, from his "Chinese house of prostitution." A short time later Ah Mow was murdered in front of this house and Baker was charged. He was acquitted, moving the judge to remark that "He was sorry he could not conscientiously agree with the verdict. He then told the prisoner he was discharged, that he had escaped by the skin of his teeth, and he hoped that he would take care never to be brought up on a similar charge."

In 1933 this building was constructed. On the Barkerville fire insurance map of 1934 it is described as a "sporting house," a brothel. A 1930s miner visiting Barkerville pointed out the house and said, "See that place? That was a sporting house. Cold Ass Mary ran it. She didn't do none of that stuff though. She had five, six girls who worked for her." And smiling, "Ya, Cold Ass Mary."

Mary, or Marie, was Marie Roth, born Marie Poffenroth, likely in Canada. At age 22 she went to Hyder, B.C., and under the alias Marie Smith, housewife, rented the Ocean View Hotel for the sum of $75 per month. The agreement was to terminate May 1932. In the winter of 1934 she showed up in Barkerville, buying this building on lot 65.

By all acounts she was well liked. Her establishment is fondly remembered by more than a few former Barkervillians. Obviously aware of her delicate standing in the community, she donated to worthy causes.

Marie stayed until about the end of World War II, for in 1944, 45 and 46 she still owned the property but was in arrears with taxes. In 1946 she had moved to Comox, B.C. There her trail grows cold. But memory lingers on with oldtimers who pause here and smile.

Several other women ran similar businesses here and in Wells in the new rush of the 1930s, including a black woman by the name of Snowball, and two Wellsite ladies of the town who went by the names Zip and Zoom.

Barkerville buildings continue to give up their secrets. Recently curator Bill Quackenbush was rearranging displays in here and noticing a cut in the linoleum floor lifted it up. Sure enough, it was a trap door and in the small compartment were two old bottles of Scotch Whiskey and a collection of mouldy letters. Underneath the hall linoleum was a wad of U.S bills totaling $70, with serial numbers from the 1930s.

Havelock/Giddings Cabin Lot 61

This cabin represents a typical 1800s miner's cabin. The ownership records illustrate how buildings passed from resident to resident. Eugene Giddings told a survey that the cabin was owned by Henry Wilcox in 1899, who sold it to Robert Jones, who sold to Samuel A. Rogers, who sold to Alfred J. Harper and from him to Thomas Nicol, who sold to Giddings.

The cabin is now called the Havelock Cabin, after Henry Havelock, editor of the *Cariboo Sentinel* from 1868 to 1870, when he returned to his home in England. Havelock had a cabin next door.

Sandy McArthur's Blacksmith Shop Lot 60

Evidence indicates this blacksmith shop was opened in November 1869 by P. McIntee. Exactly one year later he advertised a set of second-hand blacksmith tools for sale. Alexander "Sandy" McArthur bought the tools and used the same shop.

Barker Co. Claim

The Barker claim ran from the end of Chinatown down to this point. Just a few feet in front of Sandy McArthur's shop was the site of the August 17, 1862, discovery shaft that started the rush to the lower creek. Unfortunately, it has been filled in.

At this point the Barker Co. flume crossed the street, bringing water from the hillside to the claim. It aided in stopping the fire of 1868 and in saving the Scott Saloon which stood approximately where the lane is today.

Larry Pawlowicz and Mike Hall lead their fire brigade teams in a hose carriage race on Dominion Day in modern Barkerville. Ronald Candy photo

Theatre Royal and Williams Creek Fire Brigade Lot 59

The Cariboo Amateur Dramatic Association was formed in 1865 by men and women like John Bowron, Joseph Hough, Florence Wilson and Mrs. S.P. Parker. The first performances were held in a saloon, which the association soon purchased. It was destroyed in the 1868 fire, but in the best theatrical tradition, the show went on as actors and singers arranged to share a new two-storey building with the newly formed Williams Creek Fire Brigade. The theatre was located on the second floor and the fire hall on street level.

All went well for a few years, but Barkerville's buildings had unusual problems—they all needed to be jacked up ahead of the rising silt. It seems this was not done with the fire hall, and by 1876 it was half buried. When the lower floor could no longer be used, Joe St. Laurent came along and sawed the building off at ground level, jacked up the top half, cut a new doorway and built stairs to the old second floor, as in the present facade. This truncated building was used until 1934 when, ironically, it was condemned by the Fire Marshal and torn down. In 1937 a new community hall was built; during recent restoration a new front was added to this building to resemble the original theatre-fire hall.

While this story of sawing and burying buildings may seem a little farfetched, confirmation was provided a few years ago. A pit was excavated to one side of the present theatre. At a depth of 10 feet the old

Barkerville's main street in 1898 by Dawson Elliott. From right to left: Cariboo Gold Fields office, formerly Scott's Saloon, the fire hall and Theatre Royal and the Barkerville Hotel. VCA #30861

foundations were struck and, immediately below, a thick layer of black ash from the 1868 fire.

Today's Theatre Royal presents a variety of entertainment for visitors who find an hour in the Theatre Royal a Barkerville highlight. Tickets can be purchased at Barnard's Express office at the north end of town.

The tower beside the theatre is a hose-drying tower from the1930s and contains some old fire-fighting equipment.

Barkerville Hotel Lot 57C

The building now known as the Barkerville Hotel is the most architecturally significant building in town. Its uniqueness comes from the Victorian gingerbread ornamentation and the cantilevered

101

The Heron Claim on Grouse Creek, 1867. L to R, Finlay Campbell, James Laidlaw, John Adair, Mr. Dougall, Robert Brown, John Polmere, Dennis Cain, Thomas R. Pattullo, Duncan Cummings. Frederick Dally photo. VPL #22403

Historical interpreters Howard Lobb, Dave Karmyzyn and Dave Sayer, known in Barkerville as cabinetmaker Lobb, miner Sam Duke and poet/miner James Anderson, work the gravel of Williams Creek.

balcony that extends from the building front without the support of posts. The hotel was constructed by Johnny Knott. He began in 1869, but financial difficulties delayed completion. Strangely, there are few recorded references to the hotel's construction, aside from one oblique mention in the *Cariboo Sentinel* to "Knott's new building." The building served several proprietors as butcher shop, saloon, boarding house, and then as the Brown Hotel. In 1890 it was renamed the Barkervlle Hotel.

The building is the subject of research and is due for restoration and refurbishing.

Kelly's Store Lot 57B

Kelly's General Store was built immediately after the 1868 fire and is possibly the oldest building in Barkerville. It represents just one of 20 general stores in Barkerville during peak years.

In January 1868 William Adamson sold a pre-fire building to Mary Sheldon. Her occupation is not mentioned, but she is known as a prostitute and saloon keeper, giving credence to the belief that the original building may have been a brothel. In January 1872 Mary Sheldon sold this building to Annie Millar, who also appears to have been a prostitute. Andrew Kelly bought it around 1880.

It is surprising that the building still stands, for it was built hurriedly, with 40-inch stud centers, making a weak frame. Snow from the roof of the Barkerville Hotel has several times crashed onto the general store, breaking rafters and necessitating repairs. Floor and wall wear patterns documented during restoration and research in 1983 showed that it has served several functions. Under the multi-layerd floor, for example, many 1869-1874 post office receipts were found. Also uncovered were various newspapers: the *Globe, Toronto Leader, Cariboo Sentinel, British Columbian, Christian Guardian, Scientific American, Manchester Times, Punch, Victoria Weekly Standard, Harper's Weekly* and the *Ottawa Citizen,* an indication of the occupants' reading preferences.

When wallpaper was stripped from the canvas wall-covering, a series of rare theatre posters were discovered. Although they were severely damaged by paint, glue and wallpaper, and often retrieved in tiny shreds, the park conservation staff painstakingly pieced them together and restored their former gloss and luster. The posters are usually displayed in the park information center.

Kelly's Saloon Lot 57A

This small building set back from the street is an addition that Andrew Kelly made to the Hotel de France, later the Cariboo Hotel. Julia Picot bought the Hotel de France from Lecuyer and Brun by October 1869. Kelly purchased the hotel in 1871 and added this saloon. Although the 1868 fire was the last major Barkerville fire, there were still many buildings that burned down. Fire destroyed this hotel in 1949, though the addition was saved.

Street Bridges

One of two street bridges crossed here so that the better dressed businessmen and ladies would not have to walk through the mud, water and manure of the busy street. William Bowron recalled watching the frequent horse races from their vantage point.

Barkerville's businessmen and their wives sat for this photo of the original Government Assay Office in the late 1860s. Joshua Spencer Thompson is in the upper left window, Doc Watson in the upper right. It is likely Andrew and Elizabeth Kelly with their children on the right. The present building was built with this photo as a guide. PABC #10076

Government Assay Office Lots 56 & 57

The Government Assay Office of the early 1870s housed a variety of offices and private residences. It was built by D. Cain in early 1869, and the plans by W. Bennett incorporated the Greek Revival theme, the wooden pillars reflecting the stability of European stone buildings. The private residences on the sides were occupied by Joe Mason, in the north wing, and Thomas Pattullo, in the south wing, when the building went up in flames in January, 1875.

The Government Assayer who worked here tested the purity of placer gold and ore and melted gold into bricks for shipment south. The government promoted the search for gold ore, the miner's "mother lode," and opened this office to help the search. At the time it was unsuccessful, but in the 1930s the hard rock ore was finally found.

This 1965 reconstruction is based on photographs and houses displays of an assayer, a barrister and a land surveyor.

Sin Hap's Laundry Lot 54

The predominantly male population of the mines created a need for services usually provided by women. The two most obvious were washing and cooking. The Chinese quickly stepped in to do the first, and, to a certain degree, the second. The Chinese entered the laundry business in the California gold rush when they found miners willing to pay a few cents for this service. Sin Hap operated a "washing house" at this site before the fire, then rebuilt and operated for two years before selling out and moving on. The building later became Samuel Tompkins' blacksmith shop.

In the 1930s Robert Palmer built a bootleg liquor outlet and brothel here that became the Last Chance Cafe of the 50s. The building was torn down several years ago and replaced by this structure designed to show Sin Hap's original laundry.

Louis Wylde Shoemaker's Shop Lot 53

Louie Wylde (or Wilde) had a shoe store in pre-fire Barkerville and rebuilt immediately after the fire. He purchased this lot on June 26, 1871, from August Franke, late of Barkerville, "now of Seattle, Washington." The parcel was described as being, "between the New England Bakery and the house formerly occupied as a Chinese wash house but now in the occupation of Samuel Tompkins...having a frontage of 10 feet be it more or less...for $75.00." Later in 1871 Wylde sold to Annie Muller. The original building was eventually torn down.

Wylde's Prussian patriotism was clearly demonstrated on Dominion Day. The *Cariboo Sentinel* reported: "On L. Wilde's window the colors of the new German Empire, with portraits of the Prussian commanders of the late war." One can imagine the arguments between Louie Wylde and Frenchman Louie Blanc, for at this time the Franco-Prussian War was raging in Europe.

This building was hauled from Richfield in the 1930s. The construction is interesting, for there are no studs. The walls were simply a rough box covered with siding and then lifted into position and tacked together.

L.A. Blanc Photo Studio Lot 52A

Louie Blanc's Photographic Gallery was located where the *Cariboo Sentinel* office is now, but this late 1800s building provided a convenient location for the operating concession offering photographs and clothing suitable for 1870 visitors. Once again, restoration work showed this building was older than expected; it may be the second half of the New England Bakery and Coffee Saloon, the Kibbee House on lot 14B being the first half. This structure was definitely built before 1880 and at one time served as the Barkerville post office.

Louie Blanc came to Victoria from France and set himself up in business as a jeweler and later as a photographer. In 1867 he packed his cameras and headed north, where for five years he exposed his camera to Barkerville's people, mines and streets. His newspaper ads read: "Cartes de Visite, Ambrotypes, Milanotypes, Portraits in Leather, White Silk, Linen or Cotton. Views of Houses, Claims, etc. Single or Stereoscopic. Jewellery Work."

Unfortunately, few of Blanc's plates have been found. In 1872 Blanc left Barkerville and disappeared, perhaps to Europe. His stock was auctioned, and there is no record of his returning. Somewhere, in an attic, a basement, an old darkroom, his negatives and prints may await discovery—a historian's dream—providing a greater understanding of early Barkerville life.

Photography as practised by the photographers of Williams Creek such as Louie Blanc, Frederick Dally, or Charles Gentile, was in its infancy in 1870. The first photograph to attract any significant public attention was the Daguerreotype, a permanent image of superb detail, unequalled even today. It was announced with great excitement in January 1839, but each photo was an original that depended on the viewing angle to make it a negative or positive, so they were inappropriate for hanging.

Collodion, a hard, colorless transparent film that brought in the wet-plate process, was the next major development. It took a skilled photographer to prepare the plates, expose them while the emulsion was still wet and then return to the darkroom to develop the image. The advantages were a glass negative that would produce prints and an exposure time reduced to five seconds. Even so, portraits show a tense, unsmiling subject, desperately trying to hold still for several seconds.

Goldfield travelers often stopped in cities like Detroit or San Francisco to have "a likeness taken" and sent home before they disappeared for months or years into the wilderness. The photos they purchased were usually ambrotypes (which Louie Blanc advertised), small wet-plate negatives with a dark cloth or varnish backing that caused the negative to appear positive. Also popular were the faster and cheaper tintypes. A disadvantage of both was the lack of duplicate prints, like the modern Polaroid, but tintypes were soon being exposed in special multi-lensed cameras producing enough copies for the whole family. Although most tintypes were crude, a skilled photographer could produce striking photos. Tintypists prospered as late as the 1930s in North America.

Dr. Jones, Dentist Lot 51A

Dr. William Allen Jones, a 42-year-old black, came here in 1875 to open this dentist shop. He lived here with his younger brother, Elias T. Jones, both of whom had been educated at Oberlin College in Ohio. Their father had bought his freedom in North Carolina and tried to establish a school for black children. Three times he was burned out by whites. They then moved to Oberlin where four sons graduated from college. Three came to British Columbia in the wave of black immigration in 1858. John Jones taught on Salt Spring Island. Elias eventually went back to the U.S.A., but William stayed here in Barkerville. No licence was required to practise dentistry until 1886. Jones applied quickly under the new act and was an early licencee.

The shop is a reconstruction of William Rennie's shoe store. He opened for business six days after the 1868 fire and sold out in 1872.

St. George's Saloon Lot 50

This building was constructed in 1898 by the Johnson brothers of Quesnel on the site of an earlier hotel and saloon, the St. George's. During the 1930s, when Tommy Nicol ran the establishment, it was known as the Nicol Hotel.

Madam Fanny Bendixon's Saloon and Boarding House Lot 50A

If you come to Barkerville as the day wanes, when your only company are the ravens stalking the boardwalks, there would be little doubt in your mind that the town harbors ghosts. Imagination? Perhaps. But consider this building, Madam Fanny Bendixon's Saloon and Boarding House.

Originally built across the street by the Kwong Lee Company, it saw service as a residence and then as a butcher shop until occupied by Madam Bendixon from 1880 to 1898. About the time of Bendixon's death in 1898, a second floor was added, and then in 1915 the Sing Kee Company moved the building up the street into Chinatown. Several years later the building was moved again, to this location, as an annex for the Nicol Hotel. Ceiling paper that droops and curls dates to 1929. For some reason the last occupant altered the building's stairways and doors so that there is no entrance or exit from the second floor. It is, we are told, vacant.

But in the back there is a window, draped with a tattered, decaying lace curtain. And in the window, some say, a young woman appears, looking across to the Kelly House offices. The young woman has been seen by four researchers, independently. You may not see this elusive second-floor lady, but at a quiet moment you might notice the curtain at that back window move.

Dr. Watts Office and Residence Lot 49

This building was moved here from the parking lot area and restored to resemble a doctor's home and office. The side door, around the back to the right, shows the kitchen and dining area, housed in a log addition.

Dr. Hugh Watt was the grandson of James Watt, the inventor of the steam engine, and was born in Fergus, Ontario. He came to Barkerville in 1885 as a surgeon for the Royal Cariboo Hospital but only stayed three years before moving to Fort Steele in the Kootenays.

W.D. Moses Barbershop Lot 48A

Wellington Delaney Moses was a British citizen born on Grand Cayman Island or the Isle of Grain in 1816. He moved to California from his birthplace and arrived in Victoria in 1858, one of two men organizing the move of several hundred black families to British Columbia. While in Victoria, Moses operated the Pioneer Shaving Saloon and Bath House. Reverend Cridge mentions in May 1858 that Moses had "lost his wife and children." He then married Sarah Jane Douglas, a black immigrant, in December 1858.

Moses liked the ladies. September 1862 the *British Colonist* ran an item that read, "Attempted Suicide—Mrs. Moses, the wife of Wellington Delaney Moses, the colored barber, suffering from a violent attack of the green-eyed lobster, plunged into the water of James Bay...but was drawn to dry land by passersby. ...The woman alleges as a reason for her conduct that her husband has eloped with another woman."

Later that year Moses packed up his renowned "Hair Invigorator" and left for Barkerville on his own. His wife later "returned to England," he wrote. In Barkerville he ran a series of barbershops, or "Fashion Saloons," which also carried a selection of ribbons, silks, combs and other fine articles. Moses kept a diary of Barkerville life, paying as much attention to the new women in town as his accounts. He is thought to be buried in the Cameronton cemetery, but his grave is unmarked.

Moses had this new shop built shortly before his death in 1890.

Wake-Up Jake Restaurant Lot 47

This building is a reconstruction based on 1871 photographs. The Jake is an operating restaurant offering meals and service in Victorian style, though more subdued and orderly than that of an 1870s mining town cafe.

The Wake-Up Jake was named for an Irish miner, Jake Franklin, who would come into Andrew Kelly's Bakery and Coffee Saloon, order his fill of home cooking and then fall asleep at the table before he could be served. "Wake up, Jake," Mrs. Kelly would have to say. "Wake up." And so the lunch house was named.

The restaurant was run by the Kellys until they moved to Grouse Creek, when it was purchased by Patterson and Goodson, then by John Goodson; in 1873 it was converted into a saloon. Goodson left Barkerville in the 1880s for a trip to Germany, then settled in San Francisco. Jake Franklin was drowned on the Skeena River in the spring of 1870.

J.H. Todd Store Lot 46B

Jacob Hunter Todd arrived from Brampton, Canada West, in 1862. He opened a general store at the height of the rush, rebuilt after the fire of 1868 and operated until 1875, when he went to the coast and began J.H. Todd and Sons Ltd., a large cannery business.

Wilf Thompson's House Lot 46A

This building was constructed in the 1890s; during its first 30 years it was occupied by a number of residents. In 1931, Wilfred Thompson, who arrived in 1921, purchased the building.

In 1972 he told a reporter that when he arrived in 1921 the town had "150 people—half of them white and half Chinese." Thompson was an active, enthusiastic prospector until shortly before his death in 1979. His demise left the town without a year-round resident for the first time since its founding in 1862. The cabin has been left as Thompson furnished it.

Library and Gold Commissioner's Office

This building, formerly lumber merchant I.B. Nason's, houses two important Barkerville institutions: the Gold Commissioner's Office and the Cariboo Literary Institute.

The first Gold Commissioner's office was established at Richfield in the small complex of government buildings. The commissioner was responsible for recording claims, granting licences and settling disputes in his court. It was recorded in 1896 that "for the greater convenience of the public, a house in Barkerville has been purchased and fitted up, into which the Government Office has just been removed."

The Cariboo Literary Institute was formed in 1864 by a group of individuals who felt the need for a Williams Creek library. Their first library was at Cameronton, under librarian Florence Wilson. It was moved to Barkerville in 1867, where John Bowron was librarian for many years. Although many of the 500 volumes were lost in the Great Fire, the library was re-established in the same building as the post office. Some of the original books are in the Barkerville archives.

A. McIntyre's House Lot 44

In many old photographs the store of watchmaker W. Davison is prominent. It was located on this lot until after the turn of the century. This house was built in 1912.

John Bowron and his wife stand in the door of the Library. In the doorway of the next shop are William Davison and his wife. PABC #10089

John Bowron House Lot 43

When the 1868 fire destroyed the library and post office, John Bowron, an Overlander of '62, used his own money to build a replacement. For years he tried to have the government reimburse him, or at least pay rent. Officials declined, using the argument that as Bowron was postmaster, he had simply insured his own employment by having a suitable building constructed. After several years John Bowron tired of bureaucratic delays and altered it for use as his residence. This reconstruction is based on various photographs, including interior shots from the Bowron family album.

J. Bibby's Tin Shop Lot 42

Adams and Pearcy rebuilt their tin shop here after the fire and sold to John Bibby in 1871. Bibby built a log storage shed in 1890, which is used as today's tin shop. The storage shed was originally on this location but was moved back when the Kelly family built here in the 1930s. During early restoration efforts the tin shop storage building was moved forward, and the Kelly House was moved to the back street.

Bibby came from Canada West in 1871 and used handpowered machinery to fabricate everything from tin cups and gold pans to hydraulic pipe and monitors. He also sold stoves and hardware and may have made the building's fire-proof tin roof.

Hub King's House Lot 41

This was a residence and law office for Hubert King, a lawyer responsible for the passage of the Barkerville Titles Investigation Act, an act that finally straightened out confusion over land ownership. The investigation has proven invaluable to townsite plotting and research, since land owners had to trace the history of ownership back as far as they could in order to prove their claim. King, a proponent of the scheme, was also the lawyer for many of the land holders.

The Back Street

Leaving the main street the walking tour now proceeds south again, up the back street on the east side of town. Building descriptions alternate from side to side. The back street did not exist as such during the first two decades of Barkerville. This area behind the main street was the factory, the working area, the busiest area of town, alive with the movement of men and machinery, brimming with activity, a cacophony of commerce. As the bulkhead pushed the creek against the east side of the valley, the town could expand, and this back street became the area for warehouses, lumber storage and shipping.

McLeod Cabin

Kenneth McLeod and his partner Neil Wilson, the Swamp Angel, came to Williams Creek soon after the first gold strikes. Rather than dig for gold they set up a fishery on Bear Lake, now Bowron Lake. Miners were anxious to feed on something other than the usual beans, bacon and beef and lined up to buy salmon and trout at 37 and one half cents per pound.

While the partners had a station at the lake, they would have bought supplies in Barkerville. McLeod had a large house and acreage at the head of Bowron Lake. Records do not indicate when McLeod built or bought this cabin, but he was living here before 1900 and sold to F.C. McCarthy about 1911.

McLeod died in the Kamloops old men's home in February 1911, shortly after leaving Barkerville.

The Ludditt/Morford House Lot 86

This house was built in the 1930s by Harold Garden, a surveyor who retired here in the late 1950s. He left it to Fred Ludditt, an important Barkerville citizen who settled in the 1930s and helped preserve the town. Garden stipulated when he left the house to Ludditt that it not be sold to the government, an indication of the hard feelings that developed when the provincial government took over the town.

Ludditt's house is one of three private properties in town, the others being St. Saviour's Church and the Masonic Hall. In 1983 Ludditt sold the house while in retirement in the Okanagan.

Walsh Claim cabin Lot 87

Little is known about this cabin, except that it was once occupied by a man named Catlett. The cabin and outbuilding are pre-1900s.

Holt and Burgess Cabinet Shop Lot 89 (east)

Woodworkers of the gold rush era were classified in terms of the work they performed. Carpenters like Johnny Knott did the heavy, rough work, constructing buildings and mining equipment; joiners hung doors and windows and finished the carpenter's project; cabinetmakers did the finest woodwork, cupboards, cabinets and furniture, using tools such as the molding planes and treadle jigsaw seen in this working display. Wood was bent with the steam box seen on the porch.

The Holt and Burgess of early Barkerville were actually builders

Stagecoaches were the main transportation link on the Cariboo Road until 1914. This BC Express stage, with a five-horse hitch, is loading at 100 Mile House. VCA #P1017

and carpenters, not cabinetmakers, and their office was near the Bowron House. For the purpose of this display, they have been depicted as cabinetmakers. The building that houses this display is a 1930 residence built for Russell McDougall, a placer miner.

The Holt and Burgess wagon seen in front of the shop is a light delivery wagon from the 1890s.

Goldfield Garage Lot 90 (east)
This post-1900 garage was used by a 1930s mining company .

Mundorf's Stable Lot 91 (east)
Livery stables were the truck stops and gas stations of the gold rush. For teamsters, travelers and residents alike the stable was essential for providing food and shelter to the horses, mules and oxen used for transportation.

Jacob Mundorf had a livery and restaurant business in pre-fire Barkerville, the Crystal Palace Saloon, and when the Hurdies came to town, they moved in. In fact, Mundorf married Katrina or Catherine, a Hurdy Gurdy girl, likely the woman referred to by James Anderson in his Hurdies poem: "There was Kate and Mary, blithe and airy. ..."

After the fire the Mundorfs moved south to 20 Mile House, north of Cache Creek. Jacob died in 1902 and Katrina in 1904.

This photo from June 1911 illustrates the problems Barkerville faced even then, with spring floods cascading down the main street. PABC #57671

Outbuildings
Scattered on both sides of the back street are a variety of outbuildings from the 1900-1930 period formerly used as ice-houses, warehouses or residences. They are put to a similar use today and are found on Lots 44, 46, 48, 51B, 52B, 57F and 106. As the townsite develops the buildings are the subject of studies and will be used as the sites of further displays and interpretation.

Baker's Stable Lot 93
Like the Mundorf Stable, this building was constructed around the turn of the century. Joe Wendle used it for storage in the 1930s.

Kelly House Lot 50C (west)
This 1930s house belonged to the Kelly family, of Kelly's Store and Hotel, and stood on the main street where J. Bibby's Tin Shop is located. It was moved here as part of the plan to return the main street to an 1870 appearance and is used as the townsite operations office.

Display Studio Lot 98A (east)
In this post-1900 residence the displays of Barkerville are planned and built.

Michael Claim Cabin Lot
This cabin depicts a miner's cabin such as would have been found on many claims, including the Michael Claim. R. Michael and W. Michael were in partnership with A.D. Osborn in a claim below the canyon as early as August 1862. This claim later became known

as the Canadian Claim, not to be confused with the Canadian Claim on Grouse Creek, which precipitated a disagreement known as the Grouse Creek War, although it was the scene of a dispute with the bordering Barker Company claim.

Maintainence Yard (east)

Buildings from various periods as early as 1870 are now used for maintenance and equipment by the townsite In the long-term plan this service yard will be moved outside Barkerville to reduce vehicular traffic and non-period activity.

Lowhee Tool Shed Lot 103 (east)

This log building, with its unusual north-south alignment, dates from pre-1885, indicated by the cut nails used in construction. Compare the weathering on these logs with those of a later period and note the squared, dovetailed corners.

John Hopp of the Cariboo Goldfields Ltd. had purchased the property by 1896 and used it as a residence for his foreman. His office was in the old Scott Saloon. Hopp turned this building over to the Lowhee Mining Company in 1929.

Hibernia Co. Claim Lot 104 (east)

Records indicate this pre-1900 building was used as a blacksmith shop or warehouse. The Hibernia Company had a claim in this area. It was unique in that a woman, Margaret Cusheon, is recorded as a partner. Often women's mining involvement was transacted and disguised through male agents, perhaps because of long-seated superstitions about women being bad luck around any mine.

Cusheon was on the creeks by 1862, in company with her mother Mary Ann Webster and a sister.

Sandy McArthur's cabin Lot 83 (west)

This building dates from a pre-1885 period, indicated by cut nails and the gable's board and batten construction. Parts of the exterior have been fire-charred, but whether this is from the 1868 fire is not known.

Now interpreted as the residence of blacksmith McArthur, it was once the home of Ah Cow, who had an 1870s Barkerville trading business and a claim at Nelson Creek. In 1910 he sold this building to W.W. Kelly.

Myatovic Cabin Lot 82 (west)

The story of buildings and residents is still unfolding in Barkerville. For years this cabin was listed as "post-1900—origin unknown"; but in 1983 80-year-old Nick Myatovic visited Barkerville to show his nephew from Yugoslavia where he had worked as a young man. Myatovic identified this cabin as the one he had built in 1932.

Ah Quan's Cabin Lot 107 (east)

Ah Quan lived here in 1909. Extensive reconstruction was done in 1980. At one time the cabin had a porch which faced the back street.

Sheepskin Mining Company Office and Shaft Lot 108

This display illustrates a rather prestigious early mining setup. Most claims had few frills, including room for an office. Furnishings are typical, however—crude, often handmade by miners. The chair is called a Cariboo Tipster, a style developed from American Civil War sentry chairs. The balance is such that if one slumps forward, in sleep or drunken stupor, the chair ignominiously tips the sitter on the floor. The bucket wheelbarrow was used in the Slough Creek claim in the 1930s to haul gravel from the drift.

The cabin was moved from Stanley in 1960. Beside the cabin is a shaft, at one time 60 feet deep, which used a two-man windlass to hoist buckets of gravel-bearing gold, the men hoped, to the surface.

The men who operated this claim in the 1870s were members of the Sheepskin Mining Company. The Company's claims adjoined the Barker Company's eight claims on the east side. In Gold Commissioner John Bowron's 1896 report, the Sheepskin Claim is said to have earned a total of $150,000. Unlike many companies, the Sheepskin relied on its owners to work the claim; the Barker Company, for instance, hired others to do the digging. The name Sheepskin likely comes from the practice of using a sheepskin to trap fine gold. The gold-filled skin was then burned or washed to remove the gold fines.

Chinese Miner's Cabin Lot 80 (west)

"China Diggings" producing only "China Wages." That is how Caucasian miners referred to claims they considered worthless but which Chinese miners meticulously worked to show a profit. To the scorn of white miners, they would work for $4 a day, half the usual rate, share a cabin with four others and work the claims passed over by those looking for higher pay. Grubstake earned, they could then go into mining for themselves, methodically reworking old claims.

This pre-1900 cabin of unknown origin has a display depicting a typical Chinese miner's cabin.

Trapper Dan's Cabin Lot 81

Chan Lung Fong, known as Trapper Dan, came from the Kootenay District in 1921 and operated a trap line near Summit Creek, 10 miles north of Barkerville. His story is similar to other Chinese who lived along the creek. He sent money home to a girl in China, hoping this would enable her to join him. Blocked by head taxes and an immigration policy against women, she died before their dream could be realized. Dan died in this cabin in 1957.

The cabin may have been built shortly after the Great Fire, as both cut and wire nails were used. Trapper Dan's cabin was one of the first displays in Barkerville Historic Park. Although his name is attached to the cabin, a succession of Chinese miners used it over the last hundred years.

The empty lots between the Sheepskin Mining Company cabin and the Lee Chong store have at different times been used as vegetable gardens and for various buildings. The Back Street joins the Main Street here. For the purposes of the walking tour, you should now move toward Williams Creek and the bulkhead.

The Bulkhead

Hydraulic mining at Stout's Gulch in 1912. Evidence of this destructive mining method is still seen around Barkerville. PABC #10183

Spring freshets or high water following a heavy rain sent the water of Williams Creek and the accompanying tailings washing down the streets of Barkerville, adding almost as much as two feet a year to the level of the streets and making it necessary to constantly raise buildings. The Hudson's Bay Company recorded in 1871 that they had to raise their store 18 feet. Vince Halvorsen, who lived here in the 1930s, estimates there are forty feet of tailings under the Visitor's Centre.

The laborious task of raising buildings was still necessary even after the construction of a bulkhead or wingdam at the top end of the town in 1872 by Thomas Spence. The creek continued to be a problem. At its wildest, the capricious creek still tore down the street. As late as 1911 residents were pleading with the government for help with flood control. Today's bulkhead keeps the creek further away than in 1872. At that time the road was squeezed against the hillside, as can be seen in early photos.

The Bedrock Drain Company

Williams Creek miners were working in an ancient creek bed 40 feet deep and filled with gravel, water and gold. To get the gold, gravel had to be removed by a shaft sunk to bedrock, an operation frustrated by the ever-present water. The danger is attested to by cemetery grave markers. One method of keeping claims free of water was the Cornish water wheel and companion pump, but it was expensive and subject to frequent mechanical problems.

It was proposed that a drain be built along the creek at bedrock depth. A company was formed, and miners bought subscriptions to finance the operation. In 1863 a tunnel and open flume were begun almost 1800 feet below Cameronton, the tunnel moving southward up the creek. It measured 36 inches by 51 inches, timbered on the sides and top to keep out gravel. By April 1864 almost 1300 feet of the drain were complete. Miners decided to extend it another 300 feet to a point just below the mouth of Stout's Gulch on the Foster-Campbell Claim. The completed drain cost was $120,000, the equivalent of close to $2 million today. The costs were somewhat offset by cleanups which collected gold from the drain floor, which was made of blocks of wood.

Over the last century all traces of the drain disappeared, but in the fall of 1979 the Ballarat Claim at the north end of town began to rework the creek's gravel. During excavation the old Bed Rock Drain was unearthed, intact and still draining water from the claims of Williams Creek.

The Eagle Company Claim and Cornish Wheel

The Eagle Co. was staked by J. McLaughlin and David Edwards on September 19, 1862, and situated next to the Michael and the Sheepskin companies. The Eagle had a variety of owners and was not a major claim. Gold Commissioner Bowron estimated its output at only $10,000. Put in a historical context today's miners are trespassing, as the original Eagle claims were on the creek's east side, although Williams Creek has been known to wander from one side of the valley to the other.

The Cornish water wheel, brought to Cariboo by Cornish tin miners, by way of California, is a device dating from the Roman occupation of Britain. On Williams Creek these overshot wheels powered pumps that drained underground shafts and drifts and powered winches that raised the heavy buckets of gravel to surface sluices and flumes. Water was rushed to the wheel by flumes and ditches tapping springs, a creek or a lake. The water turned the wheel and then splashed into the sluice box where it separated gold from dirt, washing away the lighter gravel and leaving heavy gold trapped behind the box's riffles. It was an indispensable machine for miners but took skill and money to construct, restricting its use to companies of men who joined claims and resources to mine the deeply buried ore.

During the creek's heyday dozens of these wheels were working the creek, with many an argument ending in court over water rights and the disposal of tailings.

Canadian Claim and Gunn Hydraulic pit

The small mining operation across the creek is based on photos of the Point Claim on Lightning Creek and shows a typical setup for a cabin and shaft. The name comes from a claim once located in this area but not to be confused with the Canadian claim of Grouse Creek, the centre of a court case.

The wingdam and hydraulic pipe and monitor show how a small hydraulic operation functioned. The hydraulic mining phase was generally a period two decades after the first placer miners. It was a method used from the late 1800s to the 1930s but now banned because of the destruction it causes to streams and streamside environments.

Hydraulic mining needed great volumes of water, so mountain lakes were tapped and creeks dammed around Barkerville. Examples of this activity are Groundhog, Ella and Pinkerton lakes to the west. Long ditches streamed the water to flumes, and the flumes led to the pipe that decreased in diameter, building pressure so that the water roared out of the nozzle to erode and wash huge pits up to a mile long, a quarter-mile wide and several hundred feet deep. The gravel and water then flowed through a series of sluices with riffles which gradually separated the heavier gold from the gravel, which was washed downstream. The two-mile-long Lowhee pit at the summit of Stout's Gulch is an example. It was operations such as this that caused the streets of Barkerville to fill with tailings. .

Several pits along Williams Creek are examples of test pits made in the early days of hydraulic mining when miners sewed canvas pipe together over the winter and attached it to a primitive nozzle with only 40 pounds pressure. Low pressure meant miners had to work close to the face, where undercut banks sometimes fell and buried the nozzleman. At the Lowhee and several other places, old rusting sections of the pipes are mute monuments to man's impact on the land.

This display was built by the Friends of Barkerville and Cariboo Goldfields Historical Society with the assistance of various work programs, donations of materials, volunteers and grants.

The Morning Star Claim, Barkerville. PABC #12886

Heavy Equipment

Upstream of the Cornish Wheel and flume are a sawmill and Keystone drill, both awaiting restoration. Friends of Barkerville plan to restore the mill with the help of area lumber companies and volunteer labor. The steam mill could then be used to produce lumber for Barkerville restorations. The mill is thought to have come from Richfield.

Nearby is a Four Stamp Mill, powered by water or steam, used for crushing ore found in exposed veins. The mill was rebuilt by Iner Torstenson and came from either the old reduction works on Reduction Road or the Cariboo Hudson mine in Cunningham Pass. Primitive mills such as this are still thumping in places like Zimbabwe and South America.

There is also a Keystone Drill and a steam wagon for towing the drill. The drill was used for testing ground and is also due for restoration.

THE LAST MILE

The Cariboo Road - Barkerville to Richfield

After the Fraser River gold rush of 1858, prospectors followed the river tributaries like spawning salmon to the gravel creek beds of the Quesnel Highlands. As the miners surged north they found provisions were in short supply, sometimes non-existent. In 1861 starving miners were sent government relief supplies to allow them to escape south for the winter. Although entrepreneurs moved in to fill the need, packing and freighting costs made prices in the mines soar to many times that of goods purchased on the coast. The government realized that in order to see the mines of British Columbia develop as they should, a road was needed.

The Cariboo Wagon Road was begun in 1861, various sections being contracted out under the Royal Engineers. Most of the road was constructed by 1863, but the stretch from Richfield to Barkerville was not completed until 1865. At that time, the road approached from Stanley by way of Lightning Creek, Summit Rock, Mink Gulch and Richfield, rather than by its present route—constructed in 1885—through Devil's Gulch and Wells. Once the road was complete, supplies could be forwarded by wagons and freight teams rather than by the more expensive pack horses or on men's backs. The road brought prosperity to Williams Creek; and to miners whose claims were "proving up," the road meant they had goods and a way to escape and spend their money.

The Claims

> Noo for claims;
> And first a word about their names.
> Some folks were sae oppressed wi' wit,
> They ca'd their claim by name 'Coo-',
> And tho' they struck the dirt by name,
> They ne'er struck pay dirt in their claim.
> Some ithers made a gae fine joke
> And christen'd their bit ground 'Dead Broke'
> While some, to fix their fate at once,
> Ca'd their location 'The Last Chance;'
> There's 'Tinker,' 'Grizzly,'—losh what names—
> There's 'Prince o' Wales'—the best of claims'
> There's 'Beauregard' and 'Never Sweat,'
> And scores o' ithers I forget—
> The 'Richfield' and the 'Montreal,'
> They say they struck the dirt last fall—
> But will they strike it in the spring,
> Aye, Sawney, that's anither thing.

- James Anderson

Barkerville wrapped in snow. The clearing from early logging and fires is evident on Mount Murray. It is now covered with second growth. PABC #60221

Claim names came from miners' home towns, the names of partners, loved ones, owners; from descriptions of the claim, or the owner's hopes. From the Barker Shaft south to Richfield the claims' names—such as Mucho Oro, Six Toed Pete, Rising Sun, Perseverance and British Queen—all tell a story. The Coo- claim in Anderson's poem, actually Cow Shit, was seen as too coarse, and thus named the Prairie Flower. Anderson was associated with it.

This walk to Richfield through the claims (following the numbered provincial park points-of-interest markers in the "wrong" direction) ends at the court house where Judge Matthew Baillie Begbie made his decisions.

Barkerville 18

Barkerville was not established until the end of 1862, following Billy Barker's discovery. By the following year it was rivalling Richfield as the commercial center of Cariboo.

Diller Claim 17

Across the creek is the famed Diller Claim, which Americans I.P. Diller, James Loring and Hardy Curry staked in September 1860. After months of work the claim proved to be one of the richest in Cariboo. See the story of the Diller Claim in Gold Rush Society.

Black Jack Tunnel

A trail crosses the creek to the Black Jack Claim tunnel. The original Black Jack Tunnel followed today's creek bed and was eventually hydraulically mined. The drift or tunnel seen now is in solid rock and was cut in the 1930s. The Black Jack Claim and Burns tunnels took out $675,000 in gold by 1896. With the light of a flashlight or candle, you can walk into the coolness of the tunnel and experience a little of life in the damp underground.

Upstream from the tunnel the careful rock work of miners lines the creek like an ancient fortification or a well tended rock garden.

Stout's Gulch 16

Edward "Ned" Stout was a California 49er. Born in Bavaria, he was working with his uncle on a Lake Michigan steamer when gold lured him to California and, in 1858, to the Fraser River. He came north to Bellingham, Washington Territory, and built two flat boats for the trip to Yale, which he reached in May 1858. At China Bar he and his party were attacked by Indians. Stout, wounded by nine arrows, was the sole survivor.

After recovering from his wounds, he walked to Cariboo in 1860 and was near Dutch Bill Dietz when gold was found on Williams Creek. Stout's claim did not prove up, so he and two partners staked claims in the valley or gulch running in from the west. Their success encouraged men like Barker to try below the canyon for placer gold.

After mining interest waned, Ned Stout worked as a packer, then moved to Yale. In 1873 he married Mary Thorpe of Yakima, Washington, and had three children. He is buried in Yale.

A walk up Stout's Gulch leads to several old mining sites, including the great Lowhee pit and what was once referred as Carnarvon town.

Schoolhouse 15

During the 1860s the area between Barkerville and Richfield was less defined in terms of townsites. The road was dotted with buildings from miners and merchants. One of these was Frank Pagden's "HalfWay House" at the mouth of the gulch. In 1871 the *Cariboo Sentinel* recorded that Pagden's house had been converted into a schoolhouse, the location being convenient for children from both Richfield and Barkerville.

Gopher Holes 14

These "Gopher Holes" are the diggings of the legendary Cariboo gopher, *Gopher giganticus Caribooi,* which—like the waterwheel Squirrel, the sidehill gouger and the creeping carnivorous conifer—is worth watching for. The more pedantic will insist, though, that the holes are where a miner ran a test lead, believing that gold still remained in rock close to the surface.

Discovery Claim 13

The Gold Fields Act of 1859 specified that claims, except in unusual circumstances or terrain, were to be "100 feet square." The discoverers of a creek were allowed two claims of normal size.

The first claims on Williams Creek were staked here, along the outcropping of bedrock below the road. Although the creek was named for William "Dutch Bill" Dietz, the Williams Creek discovery claim was registered with the gold commissioner in Williams Lake in May 1862 "in favor of P. Keeman, James Costello and John Metz." In August M. Brown and M.J. Collins were added.

Looking down Williams Creek at the Black Jack flume. The road to Richfield is in the foreground and Stout's Gulch buildings in the background. PABC #M-F-303

Later a note was entered in the record book indicating that W. Dietze, M. Burns, C. Good, F. Brumiller and J.H. Miller had recorded five claims with Constable H. Hose who neglected to pass them on to Gold Commissioner Nind. None was a heavy producer of gold.

Black Jack Canyon 12

This steep-walled section of canyon was a hazardous place where horse-drawn freight wagons rubbed against pack trains and tempers flared. The gulch below the road was the creek's course when miners arrived. Having been diverted by hydraulic mining, the creek is now only a trickle.

Rerouting of Williams Creek 11

When facing Barkerville, you will notice a hill rising between the creek's old course, which you have followed through Black Jack Canyon, and the present course. In the 1860s, when the creek's riches were discovered, the hill was part of the larger ridge to the east. The eastern gully where the creek now flows did not exist. Miners discovered that the ancient channel had run to the east before being dammed by glacial deposits, so they removed the entire hillside to get at the gold. The resulting cut was known as the Black Jack Cut, and it eventually diverted the main portion of Williams Creek to the east. A walk along this new creek will take you to many old workings.

Richfield was the first of the four towns which grew up along Williams Creek. Despite most of the population's moving to Barkerville, it remained the government center for many years. This photo was taken by L.A. Blanc in 1867. PABC #61939

Beef and Bacon 10

The large flat near the road leading to the Richfield cemetery was the site of the slaughter house of Messrs. Van Volkenburgh & Co., a partnership developed to supply miners with meat, and reap the rewards. The partnership is described in the Gold Rush Society section under Cattle Drovers.

Abbott and Jourdan Claim 9

Miners digging along Williams Creek found a layer of hard blue clay they assumed to be bedrock. Above this layer the pay was meager, so the creek was dubbed "Humbug Creek." Ivel "Long" Abbott, six foot six inches in his stocking feet, and William Jourdan staked a claim here anyway. One day Jourdan headed to town and Abbott decided to dig through the clay. When Jourdan returned, Abbott showed him 50 ounces of gold. The secret was out, and now the Williams Creek rush was really on.

When winter came Abbott took his $40,000 share to Victoria, where he lost it all on gambling and drinking sprees. He once entered a saloon and threw $20 gold pieces at the bar mirror until it shattered. Back on Williams Creek his line of credit was soon exhausted, and he lived off the good graces of friends and gamblers who would buy him drinks. Eventually, he wandered up to the Cassiar gold country to try again, but never again did he have the success he did below the hard blue clay on Williams Creek.

Twelve-Foot Davis Claim 8

"Twelve-Foot" Davis came by his sobriquet when he noticed that the adjoining claims of Little Diller and Abbott covered 212 feet rather than the legal 200 feet. Davis then legitimately staked the extra 12 feet, from which he sluiced $15,000 in gold. When Davis considered the claim worked out, he sold it to another miner, who produced $12,000. The second owner, in turn, sold it to a Chinese who dug deeper and found an additional $25,000 in gold.

Richfield 7

The main Williams Creek cemetery is at Barkerville, but here—a short 15-minute walk up this pleasant side road—was the Richfield cemetery, located close to St. Patrick's Roman Catholic Church. The church was opened July 19, 1868, with Bishop L.J. De Herbomez, D.D., dedicating the building and its bell.

The cemetery was used by Roman Catholics and Chinese. There are no headboards left. See the listings in Appendix 2.

Cariboo Wagon Road 6

This section of the road from Quesnellemouth to Richfield was finally completed in 1865. Miners had to raise money to extend it into Cameronton. Prior to this the only access was over trails.

Steele Claim 5

The Steele Claim was the richest piece of ground on the creek. When Judge Begbie visited in September 1861, it was producing 30 to 40 pounds of gold a day from a six-foot-thick layer of blue clay eight to 18 feet below the surface. From an area 25 by 80 feet the claim produced $105,000 in two months. By 1896 it had produced a total of $600,000 in gold.

Glaciation 4

The valleys of the Quesnel Highlands were shaped first by glaciers and then by man and mining. For over a century, the hills and banks have been scoured and sluiced, eroded and washed until in places the land looks much like it did just after the glaciers receded 10,000 years ago. Now the land is healing itself. After fireweed and other ground-covering plants take root, deciduous trees like willows and cottonwoods begin to grow and soon the conifers return. In a few decades stripped hillsides may once again appear as they did when the miners came.

Richfield 3

During the summer of 1861 Richfield blossomed from the gravel of the creeks. The resulting town was untidy and unattractive. A visiting journalist described Richfield in 1863:

The town comprised the ordinary series of rough wooden shanties, stores, restaurants, grog shops and gambling saloons. On a little eminence was the official residence tenanted by the gold commissioner and his assistants and policemen.

In and out of this nest, the human ants poured all day and night, for in wet stinking mud the labor must be kept up without ceasing all through the 24 hours, Sunday included. It was a curious sight to look down the creek at night and see each shaft with its little fire and its lantern, and the dim ghostly figures gliding about from darkness to light, while an occasional hut was illuminated by some weary laborer returning for his nightly toil.

According to the *British Colonist* , October 14, 1862, the town was named Richfield by Lieutenant Palmer, Deputy Commissioner of Lands and Works. The Williams Creek Grand Jury recommended it be called Elwyntown, after the district gold commissioner, but Palmer thought Richfield more euphonious and appropriate.

Richfield had been chosen as the site for government buildings because it was seen as the last of the towns scattered across Cariboo. It appeared that here, at last, miners might stay for some time, so an administrative complex was built of rough-hewn lumber and logs. But by the time the town's name was confirmed and the buildings completed, Barkerville had sprung into existence. And when the fire of 1868 levelled Barkerville, both towns were in decline.

Government officials decided that even though Richfield was falling down around them government offices such as the court house would remain. As buildings were abandoned they were torn down for construction materials, and miners scratched hopefully at the virgin gravel beneath. Soon little remained. The one cabin now located north of the court house, beside the road, is a more recent dwelling. For some years it was used by "Lucky Swede," a miner from Wells who was always able to find a few nuggets in old workings.

Williams Creek Gold 1

Within 30 years of its discovery, Williams Creek had produced at the very least $20 million in gold, when gold was $16 an ounce. In dollar value that is about $300 million today, still at $16 an ounce. How much more was found? Perhaps twice the amount recorded, for miners often smuggled gold out to avoid the "monstrous and iniquitous Gold Export Tax" of one shilling and sixpence an ounce.

Richfield Court House and Gold Rush Law

The Richfield court house stands as a monument to British colonial administration. A supreme court was established here in large part because of the desire that the mainland colony remain a British possession despite massive American immigration. When gold was discovered the British crown moved quickly and established a revised form of British rule in this land where most individuals came seeking wealth rather than settlement, riches rather than order. By the fall of

Government buildings in Richfield. The foreground building with posters is the old courthouse. Behind are the jail and police barracks, center the magistrate's quarters. On the right Mr. Walker's house and behind, Chief Justice Begbie's house. PABC #10948

1858 the Honorable Matthew Baillie Begbie had been appointed first Supreme Court Judge for the Crown Colony of British Columbia, the representative of the Queen. He was assigned the task of administering British justice in a colony of fur posts and mining camps.

As well as the Supreme Court, county courts were established for lesser cases, and a gold commissioner's court mediated mining disputes, dispensed mining licences and collected duties on gold. This frontier system of justice worked well, in part due to the determination of Judge Begbie. The result was that here—in contrast to lawless California where law and order was enforced by vigilantes—relative peace reigned. For the most part, men went unarmed; and although there were arguments and altercations, robberies and murders, they were few compared to what might have been in a place where desperate men were constantly tempted by extraordinary wealth.

This building is not the original gold rush courthouse built in 1865. This much grander building dates from 1882. When the provincial government took over in 1958, the building had been trashed. Every window was destroyed. Large ornate doors were torn down, thrown in the creek or nailed together to make tables. Two old prospectors who had wintered in the building had burned most of the furnishings. A forestry and parks employee said there was probably no other building in Canada that had so many obscenities scrawled on its walls. In frustration a visiting artist had tacked up a sign:

"Through these doors have passed the smallest people in North America. Enter, and join their ranks if you wish, by adding your name to theirs."

Now restored to its former appearance, the building is the site of daily summer court sessions by Judge Matthew Baillie Begbie.

125

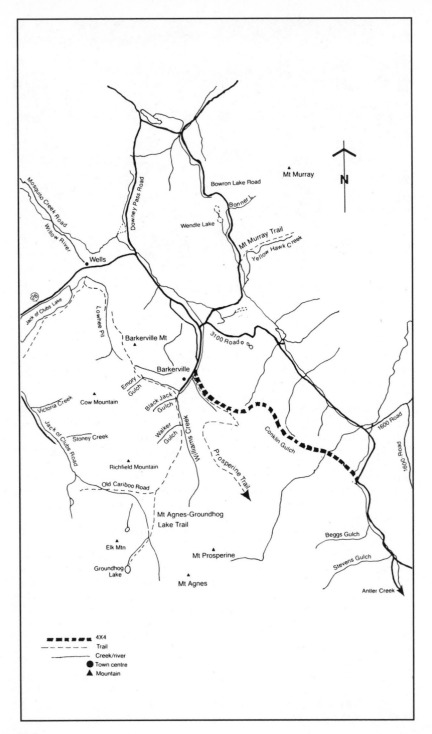

N

Mosquito Creek Road
Willow River
Downey Pass Road
Bowron Lake Road
Mt Murray
Bonner L.
Wendle Lake
Mt Murray Trail
Yellow Hawk Creek
Wells
26
Jack of Clubs Lake
Lowhee Pit
3100 Road
Barkerville Mt
Barkerville
Emory Gulch
Cow Mountain
Victoria Creek
Black Jack Gulch
Williams Creek
Jack of Clubs Road
Stoney Creek
Walker Gulch
Prosperine Trail
Conklin Gulch
1600 Road
Richfield Mountain
Old Cariboo Road
1600 Road
Mt Agnes-Groundhog Lake Trail
Beggs Gulch
Elk Mtn
Mt Prosperine
Stevens Gulch
Groundhog Lake
Antler Creek
Mt Agnes

━ ━ ━ ━ 4X4
– – – – Trail
─────── Creek/river
● Town centre
▲ Mountain

AREA TRAILS, WALKS AND ATTRACTIONS

Barkerville is only one feature of this region. Visitors wishing to stay longer and explore will find the creeks and hills easily reached by a number of roads and trails in use since the early gold rush. Trails lead to old mine workings, gold camps and towns, mountain lakes, and ridges where the whole plateau stretches before you. Barkerville site security will record your plan and keep a watch for your return. If you check out, be sure to check back in.

Barkerville Trails

The **Mount Agnes - Groundhog Lake Trail** is the most accessible historic. The lake trail will take a day, but Summit Rock can be reached and a return made in an easy two-hour walk. The route follows the final few kilometers of the Cariboo Road. The trail leads through Richfield and up Mink Gulch to Summit Meadows. Along the way you might see deer, moose, porcupine, red squirrels and grouse. Summit Rock and the meadows were popular for picnics in Barkerville's heyday. This historic trail allows you to capture a little of the feeling of the old days.

The **Mount Murray Trail**, on the other hand, is not so historic but draws Barkerville visitors because Mount Murray looms at the north end of the main street with a beacon-like repeater station on top. The route requires more of a climb, but the energetic can still do it in a half day. Most hikers will prefer to take a day and explore the alpine meadows rather than rush up and down. The panoramic view from the top extends from the Bowron Lakes south to Mount Proserpine and takes in all the gold country surrounding Williams Creek. The view alone is worth the climb.

Those looking for a more leisurely walk, might try the old **Stout's Gulch Trail**. Ned Stout's strike here in 1862 prompted men like Barker and Cameron to try for gold further downstream. The present road was built in 1879 to connect the small community of Carnarvon at the summit with Williams Creek businesses. The road climbs gradually to the old Canusa mine buildings, from a later era, and reaches the beginning of the Lowhee Pit.

Gold was found on Lowhee Creek in 1861 by Richard Willoughby, who named it after "The Great Lowhee," a secret miners' protective society on the lower Fraser. Much of the gold from the Lowhee was retrieved by hydraulic mining—the immense 6.5m pit and the extensive tailings at Wells being the result. Although the pit can be hiked, it is rough going and is better travelled by skis in winter.

Another trail in the area is the **Forest Rose Nature Trail** at the Forest Rose Campground north of the airfield. This is a kilometer in length and makes a pleasant afternoon stroll.

Richfield courthouse, 1903. PABC #22924

The town of Wells also provides interesting walks, with stops at the museum, community center, churches, Nob or Snob Hill and the Jack of Clubs Hotel.

There are many other historic trails in the hills above Williams Creek, but unfortunately most are overgrown and difficult to find. With a modern topographic sheet, pre-1900 maps and aerial photographs, some can be located, but they are suitable only for experienced navigators and hikers. For more information on these trails, contact the staff. The Friends of Barkerville and Cariboo Goldfields Historical Society is researching historic trails, roads and ditchlines and preparing a guide. Contact them at the Barkerville site for an update.

Mount Agnes - Groundhog Lake Trail

Trailhead: Barkerville

Route: Follow Cariboo Road past Richfield, taking middle fork at court house, up to Summit Rock. Follow ditch line on south side of meadow or road up Jack of Clubs Lake to Groundhog Lake. The Cataline Trail, still being marked, heads west over the saddle to the Cariboo Road. An eastward trail crosses Bald Mountain to the Proserpine area. Check with Friends of Barkerville for route information before proceeding.

Return distance: 12 km

Elevation gain: 490 m

Time to Allow: 5 hours

Map: Rough trail map from Parks Branch or N.T.S. Wells, 93 H/4

Aerial photo: BC5393 No. 057

Yellowhawk Creek - Mount Murray Trail

Trailhead: Km 5 on Bowron Lake Road. Gravel pit on right. Trail begins on pit's left or north side.

Route: Up Yellowhawk Creek. Take left fork (after about one hour).

Mount Murray is a good two-hour climb to the north of Barkerville, offering a wide-angle view of the gold rush creeks.

At cabin cut across meadows to Mount Murray's slopes.
Return Distance: 7 km
Elevation Gain: 680 m
Time to Allow: 4 hours
Map: N.T.S. Spectacle Lakes, 93 H/3

Stout's Gulch Trail
Trailhead: Begin in Barkerville. Take Richfield Road for 0.5 km and then turn right, west, up Stout's Gulch.
Route: Up Stout's Gulch to summit and return or continue down Lowhee Creek and the Lowhee Pit to Wells Ski Hill.
Return Distance: 6 km to summit and return. 10 km to Wells.
Elevation gain: 150 m
Time to Allow: 2-3 hours to summit. 4 hours to Wells.
Map: N.T.S. Wells, 93 H/4
Aerial photo: BC5393 No. 057 or Barkerville Mosaic PM344

Cariboo Road Trail
Trailhead: Begin in Barkerville or Stanley.
Route: From Barkerville proceed to Summit Rock, as in Groundhog Lake Trail. Follow road along Jack of Clubs Creek to Ella Lake, then down north side of Lightning Creek. The road has been cleared by Friends of Barkerville but is washed out in some sections. Suitable for foot, mountain bike or skiing. Check with FOB for route information before attempting. From Stanley follow in reverse.
Distance: One-way, 20 km
Time to Allow: 1-2 days
Map: N.T.S. Wells, 93 H/4
Aerial photo: BC5393 No. 059 and No. 058

An early photo of a guiding party on Isaac Lake, Bowron Lakes chain. PABC #10145

Other Attractions

The foremost attraction in the area, aside from Barkerville, is **Bowron Lakes Provincial Park**, a 116 km canoe circuit around a chain of lakes and rivers. This 121,000 ha of wilderness is located in the Cariboo Mountains, just 28 km from Wells. It was established as a hunting reserve in 1927 and then as a park in 1961 and is named for John Bowron. The full route is a seven- to ten-day trip. The west side can be canoed one to five days. The west side has the advantage of offering several days of canoeing with no portages, whereas the east side begins with a 2.4 km portage. Although most visitors to Barkerville will not be prepared for a lengthy wilderness journey, a one- or two-day trip on Bowron and Spectacle lakes may be appealing. A circuit fee and reservation system is in effect from mid-June through September, payable at the park visitor center on Bowron Lake. All park visitors must register before traveling the circuit. Canoes and equipment may be rented from the lodges at Bowron Lakes. There are 25 campsites at the park entrance. Contact the B.C. Parks Branch in Williams Lake or in the summer season at Bowron Lake, for complete information.

See also: *Bowron Lakes, a Year-Round Guide* by Richard Thomas Wright, Heritage House Publishing, Box 1228, Sta. A., Surrey, B.C. ISBN 0-919214-77-0.

A short distance up the Bowron Lakes Road is another small park suitable for day use, **Wendle Lake Park**. This is the swimming hole for locals and is large enough for a canoe. A short walk leads from Wendle Lake to Bonner Lake.

Backroads to mining claims and logging operations lead up many creeks and into the hills. While some of these, such as the 3100 Road which begins just 0.5 km down the Bowron Road, can be driven by a standard passenger car, most require high clearance and in some cases four-wheel drive vehicles. As the conditions of these roads change frequently and travel is often dependent on weather, it is a good idea to check them out locally first. Topographic maps will help you find your way, but the most up-to-date will be the Forest Service recreation maps. The two that pertain to this area are: Quesnel Lake and Area, and North Cariboo, both obtainable from Forest Service offices.

For Bowron Lake information and registration, call (250) 992-3111.

Visitor Services - Barkerville

Barkerville Historic Townsite is open year-round, from dawn to dusk. However, most services are limited to the summer season (June to September), in keeping with the historic mining season of April to October.

Placer mining required running water. The long, cold winters, with temperatures dropping to -45 degrees C and snow piling up to 6 m deep, forced miners out of the area or indoors for winter. The town and merchants have lately sponsored Halloween festivities and various functions around the Christmas period.

Administration offices at Barkerville are open all year. There are no accommodations in the park. There is a nightly fee in all nearby campsites and a maximum stay of 14 days.

Accommodation

St. George Hotel, Barkerville
Box 4, Barkerville, V0K 1B0
250-994-0008

Lowhee Campground
On Wells-Barkerville road, east of Wells, 90 sites, sani-station, showers, pit toilets, fire pits.

Forest Rose Campground
On Bowron Lake Road at Km 0.5, east of Wells. 48 sites, showers, pit toilets, fire pits.

Government Hill Campground
On Reduction Road, above Cemetery, 25 small sites, not suitable for trailers. Short walk to townsite. Pit toilets and fire pits.

Picnic Site
Near the entrance to Barkerville town, at the north end of the parking lot.

131

Information Services

Manager
Barkerville Historic Townsite
Barkerville, B.C. V0K 1B0
(250) 994-3332

Visitor Services - Wells

The 1930s mining town of Wells provides most of the services for visitors to the Williams Creek area. There are two hotels and two motels. Further accommodation is offered at Bowron Lake lodges. There is a Hard Rock Mining Museum, and several local celebrations are of interest to visitors.

Groceries and gas are available and several cafes with a variety of fare. The town may soon be the site of a gambling casino. Wells is also the gateway to the canoe circuit of Bowron Lakes Provincial Parks, 28 km northeast.

The nearest other supplies and accommodations are at Quesnel on Highway 97. Quesnel is serviced by daily jet aircraft, B.C. Railway, and bus lines.

Accommodation

Wells Hotel
Pooley St.
Wells, B.C. V0K 2R0
(250) 994-3427; Fax 994-3394

Hubs Motel
Box 116
Wells, B.C. V0K 2R0
(604) 994-3313

Whitecap Motor Inn & RV Campground
Ski Hill Road
Wells, B.C. V0K 2R0
(250) 994-3489 or 994-3426

Camping and Sani-Station: Private campgrounds with showers are found at the Whitecap Motor Inn and at Bowron Lake lodges. There are government campgrounds near Barkerville and Bowron Lake, 28 km northeast.

Airstrip: East of Wells. Length, 762 m (2,500 ft); elevation, 1280 m (4,200 ft); paved.

Police: RCMP in Wells (250) 994-3314.

Boat Launching: Sites on Jack of Clubs Lake and Bowron Lake.

ROAD TO THE CREEKS

Quesnel to Barkerville

km 0.0 Quesnel

Entry in the journal of Simon Fraser: *Monday, August 1st, 1808. Set out early. Debarked at Quesnel's River where we found some of the natives, from whom we procured some furs, plenty of fish and berries. Continued our route until sunset.*

So Fraser named this river for Jules Maurice Quesnel, a North West Company clerk, one of Fraser's two lieutenants on his historic downriver journey of discovery.

Quesnellemouth on the Fraser, October 1865. Charles Gentile photo. PAC #88913

As miners came up the Fraser half a century later, entrepreneurs were not far behind. The first store was built at this junction in 1860. By 1861 there were two, and a couple of settlers. Then in May 1862 the colonial government reserved land here, anticipating a town. By spring of 1863 the *Colonist* reported a town springing up, "which bids to be the largest interior town in B.C." It was referred to as Quesnellemouth to distinguish it from Quesnelle Forks, 90 km further upstream, at the confluence of the Quesnel and Cariboo rivers. In the early 1900s the post office and the town's name were shortened to Quesnel.

In gold rush days, Quesnellemouth was the entrance to the goldfields for many miners. The alternative route was to branch off at Williams Lake to Quesnelle Forks and then over the Snowshoe Plateau. It was a difficult route, cursed with mud holes and deep snow.

A contract for a trail from Quesnellemouth was let in 1862, but completion of the Cariboo Road had to wait until 1865, long after the boom years for Williams Creek. But the road and Fraser River sternwheelers established Quesnel as a major river port and supply point.

Today Quesnel has a population of 8000 and serves an area population of 24,000. It is serviced daily by commercial airlines, British Columbia Railway and Highway 97, the historic Cariboo Highway. In LeBourdais Park there is an information center and museum which focuses on agriculture, the fur trade and gold mining.

Kilometer zero for "The Road to the Creeks" is the junction of Highway 97 and Highway 26 to Wells-Barkerville. Barkerville is 80 km east of Quesnel. Highway 26 is well maintained, two-lane, paved, climbing from 545 m in Quesnel to 1219 m in Wells. Grades of up to 8% make it a difficult road for heavy trailers.

This road to the mines is a journey back in time. The road is still in much the same location but now traveled in an hour rather than several days, and in comfort rather than in adversity and discomfort.

km 24.0 Cottonwood and Swift River

Downstream from this point, the river is know as the Cottonwood, upstream the Swift. The Cottonwood is named for one of the area's common trees, the black cottonwood, *Populus trichocarpa*. It is the largest native poplar and one of the fastest growing hardwoods.

km 25.0 Cottonwood House Provincial Park

Cottonwood House is one of the few Cariboo roadhouses still standing. Since its purchase as a provincial historic site in 1963, it has been painstakingly restored as an interpretive center.

Cottonwood Farm was pre-empted in 1863 by John Ryder, in partnership with Allen Smith. The roadhouse they erected that fall was described as being unfurnished and uncomfortable. Over the next decade the stopping house and ranch went through a number of owners, mortgages and liens, finally being sold to John Boyd in March 1874 for $5000.

In the meantime Boyd had been establishing Coldspring House, a few miles east, and had purchased the property eastward known as Pine Grove or Edward's Ranch. Consequently the Boyds did not move to Cottonwood House until 1886. They remained here the rest of their lives, raising 10 children. John Boyd died in 1909 and Mrs. Boyd in 1940 at the age of 89.

The Cottonwood house day book, religiously kept up to date by the Boyds recorded: *March 30th, 1909. At 2:45 today the remains of the late John Boyd were laid to rest on the bench back of the house near the graves of Joseph Ross and John A. Yates.*

Boyd was later reinterred at Quesnel.

John A. Yates died November 13, 1893, age 53 years, a native of Cornwall. He was foreman of the Big Bonanza Claim in 1880.

km 31.5 Swift River Forest Road

Swift River Forest Road follows the river to the headwaters of the Swift and Little Swift. Just past the junction is a Ministry of Forest recreation site on Lightning Creek suitable for picnicking and camping.

km 33.5 Lover's Leap

A stagecoach driver with an attractive passenger pulled in here and threatened to drive the coach and horses over if she would not marry him. She didn't, and another passenger convinced him to complete the trip. Every area should have such a leap—just to know it's there in case you need it.

km 39.5 Lightning Creek

Here at Lightning Creek we have reached the goldfields. It was discovered early in 1861 by Bill Cunningham and his partners, who had crossed over from Jack of Clubs Creek. "Boys, this is lightning," Bill said, when the creek barred their way, using an expression that meant anything hazardous and difficult. The party staked a claim up in the Stanley-Van Winkle area and though it did not "prove up," a few months later other claims did, making the creek a major gold producer. The creek rises on the height of land above Richfield and flows into the Cottonwood near Cottonwood House.

Wingdam

That there is gold at the bottom of Lightning Creek there is no doubt. The problem is the "slum"—a thick, gumbo-like mud—that flows into any crack, crushing mine supports and collapsing drifts. This site has seen many operations, none wholly successful. In the 1930s this was a small town and a major mine operation. Shafts were drilled straight down through solid bedrock to a depth of 84 m with tunnels along the creek for 90 m. Raised inclines from the tunnel went into the creek channel for mining. For decades various miners and companies tried to hit a hot spot. In the early 1960s the mine was the subject of a major stock promotion. The plan was to "freeze" the slum by injecting a substance that would make it like concrete. Unfortunately the plan failed. The shaft house was destroyed by fire on November 5, 1974. In 1993 the site was again the scene of another attempt to beat the slum.

km 42.5 Blessing's Grave

In 1867 Charles Morgan Blessing of Ohio arrived at Yale on his way to the Cariboo mines and was joined by Wellington Delaney Moses, a black barber from Barkerville. Between Yale and Quesnellemouth they fell in with gambler James Barry. At Quesnellemouth they parted company, Moses going on to Barkerville and the other two waiting, wanting to rest.

Moses reopened his shop and then became concerned when the others did not show up. Finally, Barry appeared with the unlikely story that Blessing had turned back. Moses was suspicious but had no proof of any wrongdoing. About the same time Blessing's body was found near Edward's place at Pinegrove, with a bullet hole in the back of his head. Blessing was buried where he was found.

Barry tried to skip, but he was captured at Yale and returned to Richfield for trial. The jury found him guilty, and Judge Begbie sentenced him to hang. He was hanged in front of the court house, sharing the scaffold with an Indian found guilty of killing a miner named Morgan near Soda Creek. These were the only two hangings on Williams Creek.

km 43.0 Pinegrove

In 1862 E.F. Edwards and W. "Bloody" Edwards, an Englishman

who acquired his nickname by using the word "bloody" frequently, preempted lots 387 and 388 and built a stopping house here on Lightning Creek. One of the brothers—it is unclear which—was a mate on a merchantman for 8 years, then mined in Australia. E.F. Edwards had mined on the lower Fraser in 1859.

In 1866 they sold to John Hamilton who gave it the name Pinegrove. He sold to John Boyd in 1872, for $500. There are no records indicating what became of the stopping house.

On the left of the highway is the Troll ski resort.

km 50.0 Beaver Pass Industrial Road
This Forest Access Road goes up the Willow River and rejoins Highway 97 near Prince George. It also forks east and joins the Bowron Lake Road.

This was once the site of a famous roadhouse, Beaver Pass House, built on land pre-empted in July 1862 by Henry Georgeson and George Buchanan. In 1860 they had planted a garden plot of four acres on Edinburgh Flat on the Fraser River. In the late 1890s it was combined with land preempted by George Hyde and John Peebles to form the 800-acre Beaver Pass Ranch. The road house, later operated by John's son William, closed in the 1930s and collapsed several years ago.

km 50.5 Hyde Creek
The creek is named for George Hyde, who became the third owner of Beaver Pass House in 1872.

km 52 Donovan's Creek
On the south side of the valley near a curve in the highway a small creek and valley can be seen. This is Donovan's or Poorman's Creek, the site of Billy Barker's last hurrah. His partners in the venture read like a Cariboo Who's Who. In November 1890 David Edwards, George Munro, William Barker, Josiah Rowe, Frank Hoar, John Peebles, William Ellis, W. Wormald, Gomer Johns, Joseph Mason, Ithiel B. Nason, Samuel A. Rogers and Chips Hagerman recorded 1300 ft of creek, next to the upper line of Donovan's Discovery claim. It was to be known as the Willow Company. That same day all but Edwards, Munro, Barker, Hoar and Rowe sold their shares to the Willow Co. for $1.00. The reason is not clear, but it appears they were trying to help their old friends get a large claim.

In 1892 Edwards sold his share. In 1893 James Donovan rerecorded the claim in his favor. There is no evidence that Barker sold his shares in 1892. More likely he and his partners let the claims lapse due to a distinct lack of success. It is likely that by now the cancer that killed Barker in July 1894 was advanced and that he retired south to friends at Clinton. The last hurrah was the whisper of dying men.

km 56.5 Jaw Bone Creek
"Jaw Bone" was miners' slang for credit. One Cariboo bar had a polished horse jaw hung where all might see it with the announcement, "None of this here."

km 58.7 Stanley Road (to Stanley and Van Winkle)
In July 1861 Ned Campbell found gold on a bench, and by the

Van Winkle in 1868. The Cariboo Road crosses the hillside. F. Dally photo. PABC #10505

following summer not an inch of ground lay unstaked. The workings were shallow and digging was easy. The first town created by this boom was Van Winkle, located about 2 km from present-day Stanley, at the junction of Lightning and Van Winkle creeks. Harry Guillod described the town in August 1862:

> *Got into Van Winkle for breakfast for which we paid $2 1/2 each: we had a woman to wait on us, a pretty American who with her husband kept the house, having a little boy, two years old running about. We found here also a man and his wife with a family of six, living in a tent.*

> *Van Winkle lies in a valley, shut in on all sides by high hills, Lightning Creek running through the centre; you have the sun only for a few hours during the day. The town is one street of wooden stores, Restaurant, Bakery etc....On the side of the hill at the right is the Government Encampment consisting of a few tents.*

By the following year, 1863, Van Winkle had 25 businesses. Its life was short. By 1865 the *Cariboo Sentinel* was calling it a "nearly deserted village." When the shallow diggings petered out, the miners tried to dig shafts, but they were defeated by the slum that seeped into the shafts faster than the miners' crude machinery could pump it out. Bill Hong says it met a fiery fate in 1910-11 when the Lightning Creek company bought the townsite and burned it to the ground to make room for tailings.

In 1870 mining on Lightning Creek surged ahead again as miners drilled shafts straight down through bedrock and ran drifts into the main channel with drains to take away water, and found gold on ancient high benches. Expenses were enormous, but the gold-bearing

A few miles west of Barkerville the town of Stanley grew in the wake of Ned Campbell's gold strike on Lightning Creek. By the time this photo by J.H. Blume was taken in 1899, the population was only 40 people. VCA

channel was tapped. By 1875, 13 companies had retrieved over $2 million, and a new town had been thrown up at the junction of Lightning and Last Chance creeks, dubbed Stanley in honor of Edward Stanley, Secretary of State for the Colonies. In 1874 it had 20 businesses, many owned by Barkerville merchants who temporarily moved to Stanley while business was slow on Williams Creek.

Once again the town was short lived and by the end of the decade it too was passing into obscurity. In 1885 it was described as being, "once a thriving little town now greatly reduced." Stanley boomed again in 1905, outdoing Barkerville, supported by the Slough Creek, LaFontaine and Willow River mines.

Throughout its life the town, like most of Cariboo, had a large Chinese population. While the Chinese filled many of the labouring jobs, such as ditch building, they also owned and operated many of the mining companies and business.

By1933, though, Stanley was referred to as a ghost town. After a flurry of Depression gold rush excitement, it passed into history. Now only skeletal buildings remain. Near the town is the Stanley cemetery. See Appendix 2.

The present short road into the townsite of Stanley loops around and rejoins the modern bypass in 2 km.

The trail to the Williams Creek

Dr. Cheadle, in his 1863 account of the Cariboo Trail, wrote: "The road was very rough, a narrow pack trail cut out through the woods; the stumps of the felled trees were left in the ground and the thick stratum of mud in the spaces between was ploughed into deep holes by the continual trampling of mules.

"By the road side lay the dead bodies of horses and mules, some standing as they had died, still stuck fast in the deep tenacious mud. We passed a score of them in one day in full view; and hundreds, which had turned aside to die, lay hidden in the forest which shut in the trail so closely."

The original Cariboo Wagon Road passed through Stanley and Van Winkle, up Lightning Creek to Jack of Clubs Creek then down Mink Gulch to enter Richfield and Barkerville from the south. In 1885 a road was built from Stanley through a hazardous gorge known as Devil's Canyon, to the mining area of Slough Creek. The new road cut 8 km off the distance to Barkerville and became today's Highway 26.

The old Cariboo Road fell into disuse and became overgrown. Following the lead of earlier historical groups, the Friends of Barkerville and Cariboo Goldfields Historical Society took on the project of clearing the 12-mile route, making it accessible to hikers, mountain bikers and cross-country skiers. They have since worked to have it declared a historic trail, giving it protection from mining and logging, recognizing that this is the last section of the historic Cariboo Road of any significant length. It is described in Walks and Trails.

km 63.5 Devil's Canyon

Early miners considered the new route through the slide-plagued canyon hazardous enough to earn the name Devil's Canyon.

km 66.8 Burns Creek and Manmade Lake

This creek is named for Michael Burns, one of the original stakers of Williams Creek. He and his partner Vital LaForce were also the discoverers of Omenica gold in 1868. Tailings from nearby mines such as the Ketch blocked the outlet of Burns Creek into Slough Creek and formed the small lake north of the highway.

km 67.4 Slough Creek

Slough Creek gold was found in 1870 by Joe Shaw. Within a short time it was the site of many hydraulic mining operations, owned for the most part by Chinese. Before the Devil's Canyon road was constructed, access to Slough Creek from Stanley was over Nelson Mountain. A gated gravel road leads west from the mouth of the canyon to the old sites, now overgrown. It is sometimes locked.

km 70.5 Jack of Clubs Lake

William Giles of Missouri was known as Jack of Clubs; the lake takes its name from the creek discovered by Giles, and the hotel and bar in town likewise.

High on the lake's south side can be seen washouts from the old Lowhee Ditch, devised by John Hopp to work his company's claims in Lowhee Gulch. In 1907 this ten-mile ditch was dug from Watson Gulch in Lowhee Gulch across this face and up Jack of Clubs Creek to Ella Lake, where a dam was built. The construction took two years, with the Chinese labourers working 10-hour days for 20 cents an hour. The ditch system was eventually 26 miles long.

The term ditch is misleading. They were more like small canals: seven feet wide at the top and four feet at the bottom, about four feet deep, with a steady gradient of nine feet per mile.

In one of the more notorius disputes over a mining claim and water, Lester Bonner was convicted of blowing up the ditch in several places. He made the mistake of leaving a note: "Hopp—I blew your ditches—L.A. Bonner."

Approaching the end of the lake, Cariboo Gold Quartz Mine and Cow Mountain are on the right; as Wells is approached the old Island Mountain Mine can be seen on the immediate left.

The lake was longer 100 years ago. Until the time of the hard rock mines in the 1930s the lake extended to the toe of the hill which the town is built on. It has been filled at the eastern end by tailings and refuse from hydraulic operations on Lowhee Creek, which runs south, and from the Cariboo Gold Quartz Mine.

A 1930s shot of Wells, showing the pool hall and Jack o' Clubs Hotel.

km 72.5 Wells townsite

Wells is the product of a 1930s gold rush. Before the town was built here the hill was the site of George Clarke's "Stopping House," built in 1901-02. It was a magnificent house with eleven bedrooms, porches, and decorated with the gingerbread trim typical of Victorian houses. It was sometimes referred to as the Sawmill House as Clarke had built a mill here in partnership with McIntyre. The machinery is now in Barkerville.

For years before and after Barkerville's glory, every prospector hoped to find the elusive "mother lode" of gold that had for centuries fed the creeks with nuggets and the rivers with flour gold. Greenhorns expected to find gold on the top of a mountain; the more skeptical believed Cariboo gold had been dropped by retreating glaciers and that no mother lode existed. When Richard Willoughby found gold on Lowhee Creek in 1861 he noticed pieces of quartz still attached but paid little attention. John Bowron, however, thought this had some significance and as placer gold was exhausted he convinced the government to support the search for quartz gold by opening an assay office in Barkerville. After several years with few results, it closed.

In the 1920s Fred Wells came to Barkerville, a veteran of Kootenay mines, with a theory that the quartz-bearing nuggets indicated a buried ore body. To the Department of Mines he was "an opinionated prospector, devoid of geological knowledge."

There were those who backed Wells, however, including Dr. W.B. Burnett, a Vancouver physician, who with O.H. Solibakke of Seattle and several other investors formed the Cariboo Gold Quartz Company. In 1930 Fred Wells found his mother lode and proved the doubters and the Department of Mines wrong.

The result was the immediate construction of a new town, Wells, laid out in 1933 and designed to be a progressive community. The company chose miners for their mining skills and their interest in art, music or sport. The company built a large community hall with a dance floor and gym, a racetrack and a baseball park. The result was that Wells was more than just another mining town. It was a center of culture and activity in Cariboo, with a population of over 1500.

Cariboo Gold Quartz was successful beyond imagination. Between 1935 and 1943 dividends of over $1.6 million were paid out. From the rich faults of Cow Mountain, 2.7 million tonnes of ore were mined for over $40 million in gold. The town boomed to a population of 4500 when the Newmont Mining Company opened its equally rich holdings on Island Mountain.

In 1967 Island Mountain closed, its ore worked out, unable to support further digging with gold at $35 an ounce. Wells declined to a low of 200 people. More recently Mosquito Creek mining Company tried to reach the old Island Mountain drifts from their site. The population is now dependent on mining activity and the influx of summer tourists. The local historical society is working toward having Wells reflect the 1930s gold rush as Barkerville does the earlier era.

At the east end of town, through what is called "The Strip," the foundation of the town is built on outwash from Lowhee Gulch. Tailings here are almost 6 meters deep.

km 74.5 Strommville

This collection of cabins was an early rival to Wells and was named for Harry Stromme. In 1934 Louis Lebourdais wrote of its "new and modern Antler Hotel and string of neat-built dwellings above the roadway." The area became noted for its gambling dens and houses of ill repute.

The swamp fed by Williams Creek is the headwaters of the Willow River. When Wells was at its height of activity, a racetrack was located on the flats near the island. This is still clearly visible from Cow Mountain or on aerial photographs. The mountains to the north are the Two Sisters.

In the late 1860s Williams Creek flats were the site of four milk ranches with 80 cows, producing "the whole of the lacteal fluid" consumed in the area. Milk sold at $1 per gallon. One of the dairymen who operated here for many years was Samuel Rogers.

km 75.3 Downie Pass Road

In 1858 Major William Downie, a 39-year-old Scot, came to British Columbia from California (where Downieville is named after him). He explored coastal regions for Governor Douglas and in 1859 made one of the most notable exploring expeditions in B.C. history, up the Skeena and Babine rivers to Babine Lake, then to Stuart Lake and down the Nechako and Fraser rivers to the goldfields— an impractical route but a magnificent journey of discovery.

Downie and his wife mined on Grouse and Williams Creek, where he profited, but he lost it all trying to reach gold in the soft ground of this creek delta. From Cariboo, Downie went to the Columbia River Big Bend gold rush, where a creek is named for him.

Major William Downie.
Bancroft Library photo

The Downie Creek Road, also known as one-mile road, is a 7-kilometer loop through a pleasant low pass with many signs of old placer workings. It reaches Eight Mile Lake and the Big Valley Road at km 5.2, where a right turn will bring you to the Bowron Lake Road. Another right completes the loop to the Wells-Barkerville Road.

The area immediately across the creek was the site of two brothels in the 1930s. One madam moved her operation from Stanley and housed her girls in tents while the house was built. Some of the workers were accused of not always accepting cash in payment from "Zip and Zoom."

km 77.3 Reduction Road

This alternate, higher route to Barkerville was originally the road from Williams Creek to Mosquito Creek townsite on Island Mountain. It was completed in 1868. It leads through New Barkerville, a 1930s bedroom community, and past the former site of the government ore reduction plant.

km 78 Lowhee Campground and Sani-station

Lowhee Campground is one of three provincial government campgrounds around Barkerville. Across the road is the Forest Rose Campground, named for a mining claim, and closer to Barkerville is the Government Hill Campground. (The latter is small with tight sites unsuitable for trailers or large units.)

The aircraft landing strip adjacent to the Lowhee Campground has a paved runway 762 m long at an elevation of 1274 m.

km 78.8 Bowron Lake Road
The left fork of this road leads 28 km to Bowron Lake Provincial Park. See a description of the canoe route on pages 130-31.

Ballarat Claim
The Ballarat Claim, just east of the Bowron Road, was named for a gold strike in Australia and is one of the oldest continuously worked claims on the creek. It operates under a crown grant from Queen Victoria and has mineral rights to the center of the earth. The area was once worked with a gold dredge, which sank several years ago with the gold unclaimed. (Trespassing on mineral claims is considered poor manners, foolish and sometimes risky. Panning for gold on someone else's claim is downright dangerous.)

km 79 Cameronton
Cariboo Sentinel, Aug. 5, 1863, "...but the lion of the Creek seem to be the Cameron claim; their success and prospects are fabulous. ...they now employ over 60 and in a few days they will employ over 150 men. ...the Cameron Claim has got down with their upper shaft and struck it richer than any yet. They now have it from end to end of their claim. ...no use talking of ounces they are getting it in pans full."

William Barker may have been first, but there is little doubt that John Angus "Cariboo" Cameron's claim was one of the richest.

Its namesake and major shareholder had a sense of drama. As a town grew around his shaft house, he had a huge flag made at a cost of $500, 18 feet by 30, and flew it at the top of a 70-foot flagpole. On July 18, 1863, a celebration was planned and Judge Begbie called on to dedicate and name this new town. He asked Mrs. Richard Cameron, who had been here over a year, to help him raise the flag and named the town "Cameron Town." Cameron then hosted some 500 to 600 people to a party. The newspaper observed that he could well afford it.

Cameronton rivaled Barkerville for size and influence during its first few years but gradually receded in favor of the upstream settlement. Nothing remains today except the cemetery high on the western hill.

km 80 Barkerville
Road's end and the beginning of a journey back in time, to the 1870s when Williams Creek was alive with miners.

The Shannon Mine, Barkerville. The parking lot and visitor's center now take in the area in the photo. VPL #9353

A creekside view of Cameronton in the early 1860s. PABC #10501

Appendix 1

THE CAMERONTON
CEMETERY

"One of Cariboo Cameron's men died and they hauled him up the side hill and planted him there." That's how Fred Tregillus describes the founding of the Cameronton cemetery. It was the end of July 1863, and Peter Gibson of Vankleekhill, Canada West, had died of mountain fever, a catch-all diagnosis that usually meant typhoid. Cariboo Cameron and his foreman James Cummings climbed the hill behind their claim and located an area they thought suitable.

Prospectors and miners had died before, but they had been buried in shallow, unmarked, unremembered graves that are still found in the back country. This was to be the first fixed and proper resting place.

These headboards and tombstones mark the graves in the old or pioneer section of the Cameronton/Barkerville cemetery. To one side are the more recent plots. A second pioneer cemetery is near Richfield, and a third is at Stanley. Both of these are listed following this section. Other graves are scattered, unmarked, throughout the creeks and camps of Cariboo.

Not all graves were marked. In September 1866 the *Cariboo Sentinel* wrote that the government had refused money to improve the site, so funds had been raised by public subscription. The plot was doubled in size, ditched and fenced.

At that time there were 27 graves in the cemetery. Only 18 had headboards, and 9 had no record of who was interred. In the late 1950s tourists, collectors, and thieves visited Barkerville and made off with all kinds of materials, including headboards. A few were recovered. This added to the unmarked sites. While there were many more recorded deaths, not all were buried here. Some bodies were shipped to nearby towns and to Victoria.

So here lie the men and women whose stories made Cariboo, the young and not-so-young sped to this place by rheumatism, pneumonia, fevers, scurvy, poor food, cold weather, miserable working conditions and mining accidents. Life along Williams Creek was, for the most part, difficult and demanding. Wander through these reminders of a time past and read the often brief stories of the creeks and the men and women who worked them.

Walk gently, for souls are resting here.

The information in this section came from field surveys. Additional information came from mining licenses, B.C. Intestate records, 1881 and 1891 census and records compiled on a database by The Friends of Barkerville and Cariboo Goldfields Society, on file at the Barkerville resource center. Only those actually recorded as being buried here, with or without a marker, have been included. Obituaries are found in the British Colonist, the Quesnel Observer, and the Cariboo Sentinel. The author is willing to assist anyone tracing gold rush families.

In Memory of...

Sacred to the memory of **Janet Allen** *Beloved wife of William Allen. Native of Fifeshire, Scotland. Who departed this life Sept. 4, 1870. Aged 42*

"Scotch Jenny" she was called, a saloon keeper, and when she died, "All the flags in Barkerville were hung at half mast." The *Cariboo Sentinel* wrote, "Mrs. Allen came to Cariboo in 1862 and acquired the respect of everyone by the numerous acts of kindness she performed in cases of sickness or distress. Whenever any accident occurred or any case of serious illness she volunteered her services to become nurse and friend of the miner." It was also said, "She dressed like a man, drank like a man and died like a man."

In 1863 Dr. Cheadle wrote of her as a dinner companion, "Also Janet Morris a Scotchwoman, fair fat & forty, [she was only 35] the wife of a man who keeps a store, & who came to make the plum-pudding etc. & of course sat down & dined with us."

A few months later Janet was left a widow and on June 12, 1865, was married to William Allen. Janet died when driving her carriage from her saloon on Lightning Creek's Dunbar Flats to Williams Creek. Edging away from the road edge, she collided with the rock wall, forcing the buggy down the bank. Janet died three days later of a broken neck.

Here lies **William Allen**. *Passed on July 6, 1870. R.I.P.*

John Anderson, has no headboard. He was born November 15, 1815, and died July 24, 1881. Anderson, a black, was the Cariboo correspondent for the black newspaper, the "Elevator" of San Francisco. He reported on how blacks were faring in the goldfields.

Ralph Anderson lies here, his plot unmarked. The *Cariboo Sentinel* says Anderson was "a long time miner on this creek and late in the employ of the Bedrock Flume Co., died at the hospital on August 4th, 1872, and was buried in the Cameron Cemetery on next day at 7 p.m. Deceased was about 35 years of age and a native of Norway."

*In memory of **John Armitage**, died April 21 1888, age 38. R.I.P.*

*In Loving Memory of **Dr. Thomas Bell**, Doctor in charge of Royal Cariboo Hospital. Born York, England on June 8, 1822. Died Barkerville, B.C. on August 12, 1875*

*Sacred to the Memory of **Thomas Bellings**. Late Surgeon R.H. Cariboo. A native of England. Died at Barkerville, B.C. April 3, A.D. 1875. Aged 54 years*

There is some confusion on these two headboards. Both refer to the same man, Dr. Thomas Bell, who died April 15, 1875. Bell was the "outstanding medical man of the Cariboo," according to the miners. He did not mine but attended to his practice. In an early plastic surgery operation, Bell grafted a man a new nose, after a fight, by tying his arm to his head while skin grew.

Dr. Bell was at Cameronton in October 1863 and was appointed medical attendant in November 1865. He had left his wife and children in England. While he was a competent surgeon, by 1875 the community had grown concerned about Dr. Bell. An editorial in the *Cariboo Sentinel* charged mismanagement.

"The late physician, when in possession of his health and faculties, had given satisfaction in the performance of his duties; but sickness came on him—a long, lingering sickness, affecting not only the body but the mind occasionally—and the public had not the heart to take any steps which might retard the recovery or perhaps hasten the death of an old and faithful servant."

In memory of James Bennett. A native of the parish of Pont i hyr v Fryn, Glanmorganshire, Wales, who died August 1, 1868, aged 37 [31?]

James Bennett had given his notice and was working his last shift at the Taffvale claim on Stouts Gulch when a shaft cave-in killed him. His gross estate totaled $1270. Relatives claimed $606.

Seth Berry

There are no dates or information on the marker. R.B., Thos. A., John and Wm. Berry came to Williams Creek in 1863.

Richard Berry, died in Barkerville May 22, 1908, and was buried here. He was one of the early men on the creeks. In 1849 he crossed the plains with the Gooding and Goodyear parties. He worked as a carpenter in Sacramento then bought a claim which netted $60,000. He lost money buying oats in Oregon and was unsuccessful in Virginia City so came to Cariboo in 1862. He had the Sportsman tunnel on Williams Creek and the Central on Jack of Clubs Creek. He was thought to be the last 49er in Cariboo.

James Bibby. Born in Kingston, Ontario. Died December 13, 1922

John Bibby. Born Kingston, Ontario. Died December 1, 1917

The Bibby brothers came to Williams Creek in 1871 and John took over the tin shop vacated by Adams and Pearcy. The shop is a restored building in Barkerville.

In memory of John Bilsland. Died Mach [sic] 13, 1879. Aged 43

Steep roofs were necessary to clear snow, but when the snow slid from the Two Brothers Claim shaft house on Tucker Lake, near the west end of Jack of Clubs Lake, John Bilsland was caught beneath and killed. According to the Victoria Colonist, March 21, 1879, he was greatly respected and over 250 miners attended his funeral.

Four Bilsland brothers came to Cariboo from Quebec in 1863; William, James, Alexander W. and John. Alex remained in Barkerville until after 1881 and was in Vancouver until 1922. The other brothers returned home to Cornwall, Ontario.

James Blair. At Rest. Died March 26, 1885. Aged 35

Another miner killed in a mine cave-in, this one on the Mason Claim on Antler Creek.

In memory of Margaret Jane Blair, beloved wife of John Pinkerton. Died May 30, 1880, aged 21 years 7 mos. Also their daughter, died April 19, 1879, aged 10 days

> *O cruel death; thou waster severe*
> *To snatch so suddenly away*
> *This cherished loved-one in her prime*
> *To mix among the mouldering clay*

A small tombstone beside Margaret Blair's reads *MJP*, likely Margaret Jane Pinkerton, the infant daughter of John and Margaret Pinkerton. It appears Margaret Blair died from childbirth complications, not uncommon in an area with few medical facilities.

John Pinkerton was born in Leeds County, Canada West, in 1839. An Overlander of '62, he worked the Barker Claim windlass for his first season, then spent the next 55 years actively mining on Lowhee Gulch, wintering in California on occasion. On one trip south he was robbed of "considerable money in the What Cheer House in San Francisco." Prior to 1875 he went back to Ontario, where he married "his girl bride" Margaret Blair. They settled on French

Creek, and on September 21, 1875, their first child, Elizabeth, was born. Margaret Blair Pinkerton was just short of her 17th birthday. The Pinkertons had four children: Elizabeth; a son George, drowned on the Bowron River in 1907; another daughter; and Margaret, whose birth caused Mrs Pinkerton's death.

John was left with three young children and soon found that, even with other women helping, the country was not suitable so he sent them to St. Ann's Academy in Victoria. They left a couple years later to stay with relatives in Ontario, then returned to Barkerville in 1899. John had not prospered and was living in a cabin on Lowhee Creek. He retired from mining about 1917 and went to Vancouver, where he died February 23, 1920.

To the memory of **John Blythe.** *Native of Fifeshire, Scotland. Aged 47. Died October 28, 1877*

In memory of **Jas. R. Bovyer** *of Charlotte Town, Prince Edward Island. Died 3lst Janry 1870. Aged 32*

The *Sentinel* reported Bovyer "died of congestion of the brain," three years after falling on an axe when working near Mosquito Creek. Friends erected his headboard four months after his death.

Archie Ray Bowron, *beloved son of John and Emily Bowron. Died 30 Oct. 1889, aged 7 months. Our Darling.*

Emily Bowron. *Beloved wife of John Bowron GC. Born at Clifton, Michigan, April 25, 1850. Died at Barkerville May 29, 1895*

Emily and John, whose story is told elsewhere, were married at Richfield, August 16, 1869. Besides Archie Ray, Emily had two other sons, Edward and William, and two daughters, Alice and Lottie. John Bowron is buried in Victoria, B.C.

In memory of **James Boyce.** *Died March 11, 1911. Aged 76 years*

The Quesnel *Cariboo Observer* records Boyce's death as January 27, 1911. He was born in 1840 in County Monaghan, Ireland, and emigrated to Ontario with his parents when a child. He came to Barkerville via the Panama in 1862. He had interests in many claims and mines in the area and was the proprietor of a Barkerville hotel, "where his cheery manner and genial disposition endeared him to all. So far as is known he has no relatives in this country."

In memory of **Chartres Brew,** *Born at Corsfin, County Clare Ireland, 31 Dec. 1815. Died Richfield, 31 May 1870. Gold Commissioner and County Court Judge*

An inscription by Judge Begbie reads: *A man imperturbable in courage and temper endowed with a great & varied administrative capacity. A most ready wit a most pure integrity.* Chartres Brew served in a number of administrative and law enforcement capacities in the province. To find a man more suitable would have been difficult.

When Brew returned to Ireland in 1835 after serving in the Spanish Legion, he entered the Irish Constabulary. When the Crimean War broke out he was appointed Deputy Assistant Commissary General. In 1858 Colonial Secretary Sir Edward B. Lytton offered Brew the appointment of Chief Commissioner of Police in the new colony of British Columbia. Accepting, Brew handled such problems as a disturbance of miners at Yale, the Chilcotin War—where natives warred against encroaching whites—and served as chief Gold Commissioner and stipendiary magistrate. Brew was sent to Cariboo in 1867 where, the *Cariboo Sentinal* says, he "secured the esteem and respect of the whole community by his impartiality and manifest intentions to do justice in matters brought before him...he managed to discharge his duties in the most creditable manner to the general satisfaction of the inhabitants of Cariboo."

*In memory of **Bill Brown**. Born near Westport, Ontario, Dec. 16, 1839. Died January 19, 1939*

Although Bill Brown came to Williams Creek after the initial rush, his residence here for 67 years, from 1872 to his death in 1939, marks him as one of the oldest residents. Author Bruce Hutchinson met Brown in the Kelly Hotel during the Depression years and later described him in his book *The Fraser*. "An ancient man with a Santa Claus beard was sitting by the belly of the drum stove when I came in. He looked up at me suspiciously. His name was Bill Brown, he was one of the Argonauts, he lived alone in the hills and came to town for a bit of excitement now and then. But he would not talk to strangers. This turned out to be a big night in Barkerville, for three other outsiders drove in by automobile—too big a night for Bill Brown. At the sight of this mass invasion he shuffled out of the hotel without a word, mounted his horse almost as old as himself, and rode out of town."

Brown had a claim west of Barkerville in the Lightning Creek area.

*In memory of **H.N. Brown**. Born November 12, 1849. Died October 12, 1896. A native of Germany. R.I.P.*

Henry Nicolas Brown was the father of a large family and with his wife Mary operated a hotel in Richfield.

*RIP **George Buie**. Expired Nov. 2, 1869*

*In loving memory of **John A. Cameron**. Died Nov. 7, 1888. Aged 68 years. A native of Glengarry, Ontario*

Cameron struck it rich on Williams Creek, then returned east with his wealth. Later, old and destitute, he returned to try again. Success eluded him. He found a resting place where 25 years before he had begun a cemetery with the body of Peter Gibson.

*In loving memory of **Joseph Campbell**, 1873 - 1936. **Maude**, 1882 - 1936*

*In memory of **F. Castagnette** native of Rappalo, Italy. Died July 4, 1882. Aged 44. At Rest*

Castagnette's obituary in the *Colonist* says that he was prosperous and, "in 1868 was a wealthy merchant in Barkerville, and one of the heaviest losers in the fire. ...The funeral was held in the Theatre Royal, the Methodist church being too small." He was described as, "an upright man of singularly amiable disposition and his early death is greatly deplored." The headboard was made by Barkerville carpenter Johnny Knott.

*In memory of **L. Coutts** 1898*

There was an Alexander Coutts recorded in the 1881 and 1891 census; born about 1838, a Scot and a miner.

*In memory of **W.J. Crawford** of Port Hope, C.W. Died July 22, 1864. Aged about 30 years*

Oliver Cromwell. "An old and well known miner, died on Tuesday morning at the Royal Hospital," *Cariboo Sentinel*, April 12, 1873. He was a native of the United States, aged about 40. Cromwell's marker is likely one of those stolen when the cemetery in Barkerville was vandalized during the late 1950s. Cromwell was on the creeks in 1863.

*Sacred to the memory of **Samuel Daniels**. Native of Milton Abbot, Devonshire, England. Aged 32 years, who met with his death on the 15th of June 1864 by accident while working in the Prairie Flower Ore Claim*

Samuel bought his mining licence April 29, 1863.

Sacred to the memory of Felix Daoust, native of [Coteau Landing] Quebec, Canada. Died at Barkerville 8th of August 1872. Rest in Peace
Daoust was a Cariboo Lodge Mason. His estate totaled $1131, with no relatives.

Sacred to the memory of W.F. Davidson. Native of Wales. Died at Barkerville, B.C. September 25, 1864
Applied for his mining licence April 30, 1863.

In memory of Robert Davis Native of England. Died Sept. 4, 1891. Age 59
The 1881 census indicates Davis was a miner, German born, of a Welsh father and German mother who likely arrived in '64.

Dick Dekker

Joseph Denny. September 5, 1891. Aged 68 years
Saloon-keeper Joe Denny, an Irishman, was active in community affairs and Captain of the Williams Creek Fire Brigade. His saloon is in Barkerville. He died the day after Robert Davis. The census indicates he was 59, not 68, in age.

In loving memory of George Alfred [Dow], beloved husband of Fanny Dow. Born at Walsea Island, Essex, England on May 5, 1842. Died at Barkerville, B.C. January 2 1902. Asleep in Jesus
In 1876 Dow was mining on Antler Creek.

Sacred to the memory of John Dunn native of Wick, Glanmorganshire, South Wales, who died at 1 o'clock a.m. Oct. 6, 1863. Aged 24 years. Nghanoel ein bywyd yr ydym mewm angau
Dunn was one of the Welshmen whose mining expertise from their native Wales and later California brought such machinery as the Cornish water

wheels to Williams Creek. The Welsh phrase on his tombstone is directly translated as, *In the midst of life we are in sorrow*, or more freely, *In the midst of life we are in death*, credited to a monk named Notker in 912 AD.

Sacred to the memory of Donald Easter. Native of Vanklee____l, C.W. Died 21 Sept. 1864. Aged 29 years
Easter's home town is likely Vankleekhill, where Peter Gibson also hailed from.

In Memory of David Edwards. Died April 26, 1911. Aged 87 years. A native of Machymlleth, Montgomeryshire, Wales
Edwards came to Cariboo in 1863. He was a shoemaker and lived several years in Stanley and Van Winkle. He was active in many claims and in the 1890s was a partner of Billy Barker and several others in the Willow and Discovery Claims on Poorman's Creek near Beaver Pass. In 1908 he had his photo taken on the Barkerville Government agent's office boardwalk with several other old-timers. David, dressed in his long black coat and vest, with his top hat, stands several inches shorter than his companions.

Stranger, respect the Memory of Harry Edwards Esq. Age 33. Died August 8, 1873. R.I.P.
Edwards was on the creeks by 1863 when he joined other miners in petitioning for a mining board.

In memory of [John] Rosser Edwards native of Tredegar, Monmouthshire, South Wales, who died 29 Nov. 1867, aged 45 years
A successful miner, Edwards left an estate of $3562. He drowned in a mine shaft.

In loving memory of Ener Enerson. Died Feb. 15, 1903. Age 38 years
Recorded in the *Ashcroft Journal* as Ens. Ennisson, this man was killed

on the Mollie Murphy claim at Slough Creek Feb. 9 when a bucket fell and crushed him. A Wisconsin Swede, he had been in the area eight years and was considered one of the area's best miners.

*In memory of **Julius H. Franklin** of the Island of Jersey. Died June 13 [15?], 1870. Aged 23 years*

Young Julius came to Cariboo in 1863 at 17 and mined on Grouse Creek. He died when he fell down a shaft at the Perseverance Company's claim at Mink Gulch on Harvey Creek. At the request of the Jewish community, which had no rabbi, the Rev. Thomas Derrick, the Wesleyan minister, conducted the burial service by reading portions of the Old Testament and gave a suitable address.

*Sacred to the memory of **J.A. Fraser**. Late of St. Andrew's C.W. Died 20 May 1865. Aged 32 years. May his soul rest in peace*

John Alexander Fraser was the fourth son of Simon Fraser, the North West Company explorer who in 1808 first made his way down the river that now bears his name. Simon Fraser died in 1862. Two years later John came to Cariboo and began business as an engineer in Cameronton. To finance his move Fraser mortgaged the family farm left to him by his father. Though his investments in several claims did reasonably well, he could not support himself and keep up mortgage payments. Fraser was a morose, poetic young man, also described as "upright and generous." Troubles haunted his life, and were reflected in his poetry. In the chorus of a song called *The Broken Miner* we hear his growing dismay.

> *Then let our chorus loudly ring,*
> *The Broken Miner's lot I sing,*
> *Most bitter is the lot indeed*
> *Of him who cannot find the "lead"*

Fraser could not find the lead. The farm mortgage was foreclosed, a love affair fell apart and on a spring day in 1865 he slashed his wrists and

jugular. Friends found him and tried to save his life, but it was too late. The following day one of the claims he had heavily invested in struck a rich lead and brought good returns to investors, but John Fraser's Mason brethren and "the largest concourse of friends ever before assembled in Cariboo for such a purpose" were laying him to rest.

*In loving memory of **Maria Catharina Fraser**. Nee: M.C. Brown. Born November 27, 1854. Died March 12, 1904. A native of Germany*

Maria was the daughter of Henry and Mary Brown, hoteliers of Richfield. She had several children.

*Sacred to the memory of **Peter Gibson** of Vankleekhill, County of Prescott, Canada West, who died July 24, 1863, Aged 31*

Gibson, the first person buried here, was a constable in B.C.'s Osoyoos district before coming to Cariboo.

*Sacred to the memory of **William Giles** native of Missouri, U.S. Died May 3, 1869. Aged 36 years*

Giles' obituary in the *British Colonist* says he was "familiarly known as Jack of Clubs and the discoverer of the creek so named." Jack of Clubs Lake near the town of Wells takes its name from the creek.

*In memory of **Marie Hageman**. Died July 28, 1888. Aged 59. Native of Germany. Rest in Peace*

Marie was possibly a Hurdy Gurdy dancing girl, brought to Cariboo to entertain the miners. (See description in Gold Rush Society) Lottie Bowron says she was connected with the Stone and Brown families.

Michael Haggarty came to Cariboo in 1862. A native of Ireland he had travelled to Halifax, New Orleans and then the California rush. He lived in Quesnel for several years but died in the Barkerville Hospital in late April 1897. He has no marker.

*Sacred to the memory of **Wesley Hall**, son of Hiram & Maria Hall. Born Churchville, Ontario, Canada, on 5 May 1840. Died at Barkerville, B.C., 23 March 1875*

Hall died of inflammation of the lungs. He had been moved from his Conklin Gulch cabin to the home of John Bowron. He was buried from the Wesleyan Church.

*In memory of **James Hamilton**. Native of Scotland. Died 30 December 18_5. Aged 58 years*

Two James Hamiltons arrived in Barkerville in 1862 and 1863. A James was associated with the Beedy and Townsend Company in 1875 and lived in Stanley in 1880.

*In memory of **Andrew Hanson** native of Sweden. Born in the year of our Lord [date removed]. Died in the R.C. Hospital the 10th of October, 1883 from the effect of a fall in a shaft by which he broke his back and died afterward within six hours. What I say unto you I say unto all the world. If therefore thou shalt not watch, I will come on thee as a thief, and thou shalt not know what hour I will come upon thee.*

There are many mysteries along Williams Creek. This tombstone is one, for someone has neatly removed the date of Andrew Hanson's birth. Was it an error in date or did someone not want his age known?

*In memory of **David Hawes**. Died June 1938*

A Mason.

*Eternal to the soul of **Robert Heath**. Left this life on May 24, 1912. Aged 74 years*

According to the Quesnel *Cariboo Observer* Heath died on March 29th. It is unlikely his obituary preceded his death so the headboard is probably incorrect. Heath was one of the "oldtimers." He was born near Chesterfield, Derbyshire, England. He spent a few years in the U.S and came to Barkerville during the excitement of

1862-64. He was active in mining until he died.

Jessie Heatherington "Scotch Lassie" Died in Richfield 1863

Jessie's story is that she was married to a drunkard who included her in his drinking. She left him but was later found murdered in her Richfield cabin. Dr. Thomas Bell, the coroner, found that she had been smothered, while in a "high state of intoxication."

*In memory of **William Hill** native of Nottingham, England. Died 23 Oct. 1869. Aged 37*

The *Cariboo Sentinel* said Bill Hill had been feeling ill for a year and was on his way to Williams Creek for a change of air when he died at Cottonwood. He had been in Canada since 1857 and British Columbia since 1863. Bill was a house painter and painted scenery for the Cariboo Amateur Dramatic Association. The Fire Brigade, of which he was an active member, turned out in uniform and followed the funeral procession.

*Sacred to the memory of **William Hitchcock**, late government assayer, Barkerville, Cariboo. Born in London, Eng., Jan. 15, 1824. Departed this life Sept. 9, 1877. May he rest in peace*

Hitchcock was an Assistant Refiner at the B.C. Government Mint in New Westminster and served on city council before coming to Cariboo in 1869.

*IHS. In loving memory of **Isabella Hodgkinson**, aged 66 years. Died Oct. 5, 1911. Sleep, Bella, Sleep. In God We Trust*

Bella Hodgkinson was a washerwoman and boasted that she was the earliest riser on the creek. Her husband Bill agreed and would plead with her, "Sleep, Bella, Sleep." When the morning mists of Williams Creek no longer echoed with the clatter of Bella's tubs, Bill made a final plea for her with the words, "Sleep, Bella, Sleep," on her headboard.

William Hodgkinson, Bella's husband, was born in Simcoe County, Ontario, and came to B.C. in 1860 at the age of 16. He arrived on Williams Creek in June 1862 and worked on a variety of claims, sometimes for others, sometimes for himself. He was working the windlass of the Cameron claim when gold was struck.

After he quit mining, Billy sold wood and ran a dairy, carrying milk through the town in large tin jugs lashed to his horse. He was a Cariboo Hospital trustee and Captain of the fire brigade in 1905.

*In memory of **Christopher Hoffsommer**. Native of Germany. Died July 23, 1888. Age 59*

Charles Wesley House *native of Syracuse, New York. Born August 3, 1834. Died May 22, 1913. At Rest*

Charlie House came to Williams Creek in the late 1860s and was described as "one of the handsomest and wittiest men on Williams Creek." For years he worked a claim on Conklin Gulch, and later on Jack of Clubs Creek. In 1885 he established the House Hotel, now part of reconstructed Barkerville.

*Sacred to the memory of **Margaret House**. Born Germany, May 30, 1854. Died Dec. 12, 1939. At Rest*

Margaret House, nee Ceise, came to Barkerville in 1875 from San Francisco with her sister Jeanette Houser and Jeanette's husband John. She married Charles Wesley House (thereby creating some confusion in surnames for researchers), and together they ran the House Hotel. See above and House Hotel in Barkerville.

*In memory of **Charles Wesley House**. Died August 4, 1917. Age 33 years*

Wesley was one of two sons of Margaret and Charles House.

*In loving memory of **Jeanette Houser**. 1840-1933. Mother*

Jeanette Ceise, born in Germany [in 1849 according to the census] married John Houser in San Francisco, though they appear to have known each other previously in Barkerville. By 1881 they had three sons and one daughter. Two sons mined in the area most of their lives. She died December 2 in her Barkerville home. See Margaret House, above, and the Houser House at the south end of Barkerville.

Edward Housser. Departed this life. Died June 16, 1926. Age 41

*In memory of **William Hugill**. Late of Fullerton, Canada West, who died Aug. 31, 1863, aged 25. Blessed are the pure in heart, for they shall see God. Inscribed as a token of ESTEEM by his Overland companions*

Young Bill Hugill was an Overlander of 1862. The 1863 season found many of them searching for gold and many of them ill. Dobson Prest wrote his brother in 1864 and said, "Nearly all the overlanders were sick in Cariboo last season. There were only 5 or 6 who escaped disease. Physicians say that the hardships they suffered on the overland was the cause. The man Burden that beat his horse to death, died on Williams Creek, also William Hugill. David Byers was put in hospital by J. Halpenny the day Jo. left, Byers having been ill all Summer and so reduced that there is no hope of his recovery. Joseph Huff [Hough], has been sick on Williams Creek for a long time, sometimes better sometimes worse . . . he was forced to go to hospital."

Hugill's family and descendants had no idea how or where he died until this grave marker appeared on a CBC television show in 1972.

*To the memory of **George Issac**. Native of Ireland. Died September 16, 1919. Age 86 years*

George Issac was born in Ireland in 1833 and came to Canada with his family in 1843, one of many families escaping the potato famine and poverty. In Canada West he was a woodworker and built corduroy roads, but in 1862 he left for the goldfields. He was described as being 6'4" tall, 200 pounds and two axe handles wide across the shoulders, "built as solidly as a stone outhouse with the door shut." Issac arrived in Barkerville in 1864 where he operated a sawmill on Conklin Gulch. In the 1880s he explored the Bowron Lake country, where Issac Lake is named for him, and operated claims on Stewart, Antler and Big Valley Creeks.

Andre Jacquemond. Died in November 1874, at age 61, a native of Carouge, Canton of Geneva, Switzerland. He was a watchmaker by trade and had a business here in Barkerville for the last four years.

In memory of George Johnston. Native of Colchester County, N.S. Died May 7, 1865, aged 36 years

Johnston came to Barkerville in 1864. In reporting his death the *Colonist* wrote that Johnston, "died on Lowhee Creek of a disease, called by Dr. Brown who attended him, the 'gum-boot gout.'" "Gum-boot gout" was likely the affliction later called "Trench Foot," which often affected trench-bound troops in World War I. The feet, wet and cold, suffer injury similar to frostbite. Skin becomes swollen and numb and begins to slough. If the cause persists the seriousness of the malady increases. Should the cold continue, the feet can begin to rot and become gangrenous. In an area of primitive medical facilities, gangrene or amputation could easily mean death.

In memory of W.A. Johnston Native of Huntingdon, C.W. Born October 1, 1841. Died R.C. Hospital, September 8, 1904
A Mason.

In memory of Robert Jones. Died March 21, 1920

Jones came to Cariboo in 1886 and was employed by merchants Joseph Mason and later Samuel Rogers. He was born in Maine but raised in Ontario. He moved to California and Nevada, where he was a freighter, then came to Barkerville. He was a familiar sight as he drove stock to and from town.

Wm. L. Jones. A native of Beaufort, Wales. Born July 5, 1836. Died August 18, 1888

Alexander Kelly. Born March 24, 1878. Died March 26, 1878

Johnny Hastie Kelly, born at Grouse Creek, June 1, 1869. Died March 10, 1875

Johnny Hastie Kelly and Alexander Kelly were the children of Andrew and Elizabeth Kelly of Wake-Up Jake and Kelly Hotel fame. They married in 1866 and at the time Johnny was born operated a bakery and boarding house on a mining claim that Andrew worked at Grouse Creek. In 1870 they moved to Barkerville to open the Kelly Hotel. Here Johnny Hastie, and later Alexander, died. Other children, including sons Inglis [b.1882], James [b.1871], Arthur [b.1878] and William [b. 1876, see below] and daughters Jeannie [b. 1874] and Mary [b.1867], survived to carry on the family businesses.

In loving memory of James A. Kelly Native of Bradford, Mass. Died at Barkerville, April 3, 1904. Aged 33 years

Kelly was a native of Barkerville, not Bradford, a son of Andrew and Elizabeth Kelly. This is likely an error in transcription. He was killed by a native woman who clubbed him to death in her cabin.

In loving memory of Russell Kelly. Born October 15, 1911. Died September 7, 1934

*In loving memory of **William Walter Kelly**. Beloved husband of Lottie Kelly. Born February 17, 1876. Died March 6, 1917*

William was a son of Andrew and Elizabeth Kelly, who owned several businesses in Barkerville. He married Lottie Brown. They had four children. See Lottie McKinnon, below.

*Sacred to the memory of **E.[Ed] H. Kimball**, native of Bradford, Mass. Died the 31st of January 1874. Aged 38 years*

Kimball was in the area by 1863. He was an expressman and died in an avalanche near Six Mile Creek with John W. Stevenson. His body was recovered with the letters and a sizable "treasure" still strapped to it 48 hours after the accident. His estate amounted to an impressive $4948.

John Knott, born 1819 in England. Somewhere in the cemetery, unmarked, unlocated, is the grave of Johnnie Knott, the carpenter of Barkerville, who in lieu of flowers carved miners' grave markers. John carved his own and made his own coffin, but before his headboard could be erected a nephew came to town looking for John's supposed fortune. Annoyed at not finding gold he sold the headboard to the relatives of Samuel Shoemaker, thus leaving John's grave unmarked.

John Lanyon. In Loving Memory of, who died at Barkerville June 18, 1900. Aged 62 years

The 1881 census recorded Lanyon as being born in England in 1840.

*Sacred in Memory of **Frances Eleanor Lee**, 5 days. Died June 14, 1869*

In memory of **Griffith Lewis** native of Pulleg, Bre_conshire, South Wales, who died 12 April 1867, aged 31 years

Lewis was on the creeks by 1863. The *Cariboo Sentinel* records that he died in the Williams Creek Hospital of "inflammation of the bowels." The hospital's charge of $500 for medical attention prompted a letter to the editor who said this was "outrageous even for Cariboo." His estate was worth several thousand dollars, which he had made in Cariboo.

James Lindsay. Late Qtr Mastr. Sergeant, Royal Artillery. Died Feb. 17, 1890, aged 82. May his soul rest in peace

Lindsay was Richfield's constable and jailer in the 1870s, though it is said he seldom locked the door. He was known as "Whispering Jimmie," for his gossip mongering when under the influence of Barkerville's fermented brews.

*In memory of **Mathew Lynch**. Born March 18, 1832 to burial January 20, 1874. Aged 42 years*

Born in Ireland, Lynch came to Cariboo a naturalized American. He was working on the Russell-Robinson Co. claim on Lowhee Creek when, after a visit to the Richfield store, he became lost and exhausted. He died from exposure on the Lowhee Trail, just a half mile from his cabin. His estate amounted to only $80.

*In loving memory of **Jeanette M. McArthur**. Born Barkerville, B.C. September 5, 1879. Died December 3, 1960*

William G. McCormick lies in an unmarked plot. Family records indicate he came to Barkerville in 1875, following the success of his brother Thomas, leaving his wife in Pinkerton, Ontario, to try and relieve himself of debts. He never returned. However, early records show that a William G. [Graham] McCormick was an Overlander of 1862. In 1863 and '64 both Thomas and William G. applied for gold mining licences and received mail at the Barkerville post office. Thomas returned to Ontario in 1875. Perhaps William had returned earlier and came back to Barkerville to try again. He died in the Royal Cariboo

Hospital on Williams Creek, August 2, 1890, age 49. He was Irish, a Presbyterian, and a Free Mason.

*In loving memory of **Archibald McIntyre**. Born at Lochaweside, Scotland. Died at Barkerville 20th April 1906, aged 49 years. A faithful friend and a true-hearted Highlander. Erected by his sorrowing sister in Kilchrenan, Argyleshire, Scotland. Ever so dear brother, until the grey shadows fall and the day eternal dawns, they shall behold the land that is very far off. S fhada an gladeth bho lochodha*

McIntyre came to Cariboo in 1888 after working in various parts of the province as a carpenter. He was a partner with George Clarke in a sawmill at Jack of Clubs Lake at the site of present day Wells. He died of gangrene caused by a rupture of his intestine.

This stone may have been sent from Scotland by his sister Catherine to whom he left his estate.. The Gaelic means something like "long have been kept from home."

***Marie McIntyre** beloved wife of Duncan McIntyre. Born in Germany, October 14, 1868. Died December 26, 1924*

Marie Michel was 13 years old when she came to Barkerville in 1880. At 18 she married James Stone, telegraph operator (see Stone), with whom she had two children. Stone died in 1911, and she married Duncan McIntyre.

***Patrick McKenna**. In memory of, native of Duleck, County Meath, Ireland. Died June 2, 1914. Aged 59*

Everyone was certain there could be no gold on Eight Mile Creek, but on a fishing trip McKenna and Abe Stott proved them wrong. Stott is buried in the Stanleyville cemetery.

*Sacred to the memory of **Patrick McKenna**. Died June 14, 1914. "Departed to a happier vale"*

A memorial stone for the Patrick McKenna above.

***Lottie Mabel McKinnon**, August 15, 1883 - March 27, 1956*

Lottie McKinnon was a Barkerville native, one of a select few. Her grandparents, Henry and Mary Brown, ran a hotel in Richfield. Her parents were Henry and Catherine Brown, both German. She first married William Kelly, manager of the Kelly Hotel which his father Andrew had begun. They had four children. When he died [see above] Lottie married Malcolm McKinnon, in 1919. He had come to Cariboo in 1906, and, strangely, took over the Kelly Hotel. Lottie managed the hotel, a store and a transport and contracting business. Her husband predeceased her in 1943 at age 67.

*Sacred to the memory of **John McLaren**, of Williams Town, Co. of Glengarry, Canada. Died Aug. 7, 1869. Aged 31 years. Friends must part. Erected by his Cariboo friends as a token of their esteem*

Before John McLaren sought his Cariboo fortune in 1864, he was headmaster of Williamstown County Grammar School, Canada West. During the winter of 1866-67 he edited the *Cariboo Sentinel*. When he was killed by a slide of sand and tailings at the Columbia shaft on Williams Creek, the school set up a memorial scholarship in his name. His estate amounted to $5 in savings and $10 in his pocket.

*In memory of **J.L.B. McLean** (colored) at Richfield. Was laid to rest February 4, 1911. Aged 75 years*

Johnny McLean was caretaker of the Richfield courthouse for years. Born in Barbados he was one of many blacks who came to the area. His tombstone indicates their defined status. McLean was at one time a partner of John Giscome and Henry McDame who discovered the Giscome

156

portage near Prince George in 1863 on their way to the Peace River.

Sacred to the memory of Farquer McLennon. A Scottish Gentleman
In the 1881 census McLennon was 54, a miner, living in Keithley Creek.

Thomas McLure. Departed this life April 2, 1873. Age 41. Rest in Peace

Robert McNab died at age 73 in the Barkerville hospital May 28, 1902. A native of Renfrew, Ontario, he came to Barkerville in 1862. He mined on many creeks in the area and lived the last few years on Veith & Borland's ranch at Keithley Creek. He had been ailing for a year or two and finally consented to coming to hospital. He was brought over the Keithley trail on a hand sleigh. He was married with two sons.

In memory of Duncan McQueen. Native of Halifax, Nova Scotia. Died 21 June 1866. Aged 38
The *Cariboo Sentinel* records he died in the local hospital on June 20.

In memory of J.B. Malamon. Born in France. Died February 1, 1879. Aged 53
Barkerville Directories of 1869 and 1871 list Malamon [variously spelled Malamond, Malanion and Malamont] as a carpenter. He was called the Fiddler as he preferred playing his violin, as he had for the Paris Opera, but work for violinists was rare in gold camps. He kept his soul's music alive by teaching violin to children and made his living with a hammer and saw.

When he was dying in the Royal Cariboo Hospital an old friend, Captain O.G. Travaillot, lay next to him. Each knew he could not last the night so they made a wager of fifty cents on who would die first. As the night waned and morning crept down the creek, Malamon's voice rang out, "Captain Travaillot. You win. I lose. I die now," and his head dropped. Malamon's win was marginal, for the next day Travaillot died. See Travaillot below.

John Malcolm. According to early lists of cemetery plots, Overlander John Malcolm is buried here, though his tombstone has disappeared. Malcolm was an Overlander who spent the winter of 1862 at Fort Edmonton, where he sluiced the Saskatchewan River for gold. He came to Barkerville the next year, where he became involved with the Wessels Co. claim. Later he staked land near Enderby beside fellow Overlanders Fortune, Dunn and Burns but returned to the creeks. For the last years he had mined near Quesnelle Forks and Keithley Creek.

In early July friends encouraged him to come to the Williams Creek hospital. Within four days of his arrival he died, July 14, 1913.

In loving memory of Joseph Mason, died Dec. 2, 1890, aged 51 years. At rest until the day break and the shadows flee away
Mason came to Barkerville in 1866 and in two years was a partner in the Antelope Restaurant with John Daly. They later became general merchants. The Mason and Daly General Store has been reconstructed and stocked in Barkerville. Mason was elected to the Provincial Legislature and died during his first term in office. He left a widow, Ada, and six children. Ada married government assessor John Stevenson in 1898. He died in 1919.

In memory of Wm. L. Mitchell of St. Mary's, C.W. Gone to his reward. Died 24 May 1867. Aged 32
William Land Mitchell was a newspaper man with part ownership of the *British Colonist* and then the *Evening Express and Telegraph,* both of Victoria, B.C. In 1867 he closed his Victoria businesses and came to Barkerville where he bought a share in the Davis claim. After just two weeks on the job he fell when being lowered down the company shaft and landed on his head 36 feet down. "The flags in

town were raised to half mast out of respect...his funeral was the largest ever witnessed in Cariboo," said the *Cariboo Sentinel.*

Sacred to the memory of James H. Mitton. Rest In Peace. Died Dec. 1867 [headstone indecipherable]

Samuel Montgomery. *Born Oct. 28, 1814, Enniskillen, Fermanagh, Ireland. June 1, 1904*

Sam Montgomery spent 42 years in Cariboo, most of them on Lightning and Nelson Creeks near Stanley. He had been a sailor and had a captain's certificate, though he preferred life in the forecastle. He spoke little of the sea unless he had had more than his share of libation.

At age 82 he singlehandedly dug a shaft 53 feet deep and ran a drift 78 feet on the old Van Winkle ground. In 1902 the Montgomery Company hit rich ground and paid its five shareholders well, but Sam's days were closing. In May 1904, he was admitted to the Royal Cariboo Hospital. On the morning of June 1st, Louis LeBourdais, who wrote many articles on the area for the *Province*, went to see him. "I want you to get me out of this place," Sam pleaded. "I would like to do a little prospecting at the head of Jawbone Creek." He then asked LeBourdais to stop in later that day, which he did, but as he later recalled, "the old prospector's spirit had proved to be stronger than the flesh. Sam's frail frame lay on the hospital bed; but his spirit had gone."

In memory of R.B. Morgan. Died 11 September 1863. Aged 34 years

Richard Morgan, according to the *Cariboo Sentinel,* died in the "Cariboo District Hospital of aneurism," October 7, 1865. He was a native of Bridgewater, Somersetshire, England, age 34. The incorrect headstone is likely due to a restoration error.

In Memory of Laurent A. (Lon) Muller, 1863 - 1928, & Louis D. Muller, (Doc), 1867 - 1927. In life inseparable, in death reunited. Born Covington, Kentucky

These two Kentuckians spent the best years of their lives in the Barkerville area. They were reported "generous to a fault." Bill Hong says Lon worked at Slough Creek in the early days and later joined John Hopp in management of Lowhee, Stouts Gulch and Mosquito Creek operations. They were both active Masons.

In Memory of Rae Lucille Muller, wife of Laurent, 1885-1931. Erected by her friends

Mrs. Muller was known as the Bird Woman of Barkerville. At a time when the cemetery was falling into disrepair, she encouraged and cajoled those who were left on the creek to keep the site in repair. She came by her name for the birds that would flock around her when she walked out of the town past the cemetery.

She had formerly been married to T.F. Murphy and only married Laurent Muller three years previously, shortly before he died.

Sacred to the memory of T.W. Nordburg a native of Russia. Died Feb. 1, 1881. Aged 44 years

In the 1870s Nordburg was a watchmaker and according to William Bowron's *Impressions of Barkerville* he was a "queer character who did not disdain from the effects of Barleycorn. He was a different type from the others, more of a recluse. One of his stunts was to act as chief mourner at Chinese funerals. He would parade up and down Chinatown making the most mournful sounds and weeping copiously. For this, it was said, he received the sum of five dollars and a skinful of booze, and one would think by his actions, that advance payment was always made in booze."

Nordburg was here with his brother, Daniel. In the 1881 census he is recorded in Richfield, age 49, born in Russia, Lutheran and a miner. In 1905 he preempted land at Farwell Canyon on the Chilcotin River.

Charles Patrick O'Neill was a Barkerville blacksmith. He died in the winter of 1886-87 when an express horse kicked him across the shop onto a pointed stick. His family is described at his shop on Main Street.

John Oswick is buried here, his plot unmarked. Oswick was found dead in his Summit Creek cabin near the beginning of October 1913. According to the Quesnel *Cariboo Observer* he was "a well-known miner and prospector of Barkerville."

Aged about 60 at the time of his death, Oswick was a native of Wimdom, Norfolk Co., England. Mrs. Lou Muller also refers to his grave. (See Albert Smith.)

*Sacred to the memory of **Joseph Park** barrister-at-law. Native of Lancashire, England. Died 26 Jan. 1877. Aged 49 years*

The creeks and streets were lined and crisscrossed with flumes (dangerous open wooden ditches), and it was not uncommon for men to tumble in. Few emerged unscathed. Park, a lawyer, fell in a flume when drunk and was so badly injured that he died the next day. Park was one of the town's bad actors, a man "cursed by demon rum." Ejected from the Gold Commissioner's office for drunkenness three times and reprimanded by the editor of the *Cariboo Sentinel* for his behavior, his fate came as no surprise.

*Sacred to the memory of **S.P. Parker** Native of Wellingborough, Northamptonshire, England. Died January 31, 1873. Age 37*

Samuel Parker died suddenly at his Stanley Hotel. He left his wife Catherine and four children. Catherine remarried in August that year to John Austin, a Cornish miner and a widower. They operated the Austin Hotel in Stanley and had two more children.

Thomas H. Pattullo a native of Ontario and an early pioneer of British Columbia. Born Dec. 16, 1837. Died Jan. 3, 1879

Thomas H. was the uncle of Thomas Duff Pattullo, premier of B.C. from 1933 to 1941. Pattullo was the first person to buy a building site in Barkerville and was a prominent citizen who often found a way to help the needy. In one case he raised $615 to permit a miner sick with consumption to leave Cariboo. He was associated with the Heron claim, where he was photographed in 1867.

Barkerville barber Wellington Moses wrote in his journal: *Jan 9 at 1:30 the Furnnal [sic] of the Thomas Patullo took place at 2 p.m. the corpes [sic] was remove to the Burring round a very large turnout from the Deferennce Creek ladies and gents at 3 p.m. Mary Baker was arrested for cutting and wonding an indian man and for drunkness. ...*

*In memory of **William H. Phillips**, native of Giviner, Cornwall, England. Aged 36 years. Died March 2, 1869*

Cariboo was a law-abiding community in comparison with gold rush California, but it was a rough place to live. Fights, shootings and knifings occurred with some regularity. In a drunken altercation with fellow Cornish miner Jesse Pierce at Mosquito Gulch, Phillips received a kick in the abdomen which ruptured his bladder. He died within a few days. Pierce was charged with manslaughter. He later escaped the Richfield jail. In 1871 he was reported shot and killed in Grass Valley, California.

The *Cariboo Sentinel* says Phillips died March 13 at Centerville.

*In Memory of **Gertrude Phelps**. Died November 5, 1889. Age 1 year, 5 months*

In the 1891 census Gertrude Phelps is the one-year-old daughter of William and Florence Phelps. Williams was the primary teacher at the school.

159

They had a second daughter, Ethel, age 4 at the time.

Mathew Pinkerton. *At Rest. Died April 22, 1897. Aged 55*

In 1876 he was recorded as a miner on Jack of Clubs Creek, with his brother John Pinkerton (see Blair). There are several place names in the area honoring one or the other of the brothers. Lottie Bowron remembered Mathew as a well known cheery character who was good to children. "Matt used to dance in moccasins," she said, "not much of a dancer I thought."

Wiggs O'Neil reminisced about his Barkerville boyhood and talked of Mathew Pinkerton, "an old bachelor who lived opposite us. We used to have to walk up our side of the street to the bridge, then cross over and walk all the way back down the other side if we wanted to visit old Matt. He was a nice old man, good to kids. He used to give us oranges and things."

John Polmere was killed on his way to Barkerville when caught in a snow slide near Snowshoe Creek. He was found by two friends who missed him. A good sum of money was found in his cabin along with a poke of gold which was sent to his wife in Truro, Cornwall, England. He had mined on the Fraser in 1860. Born September 18, 1835, and died December 6, 1878.

In Memory John Pomeroy. Native of Colyten, England. Born 1833. Died 1913

Pomeroy died November 12 in the Royal Cariboo Hospital. He was a native of Devon, England, and had mined in the United States before coming to B.C. for the Antler Creek strikes. For several years he had a ranch near Williams Lake, but he returned to Williams Creek to search for gold. He is in the 1907 Barkerville boardwalk photo of oldtimers.

In memory of George Pond. Native of Roxborough, Mass. U.S.A. Died May 18, 1883. Aged 51 years

Pond came to the area in 1862. When he died he was a clerk for Mason and Daly.

Pte. M.E. Porteous. 931512. 1886 - 1932. 3 Tunlc, Coy. C.E.F. "Lest we forget."

Milton E. Porteous was just 46 years old, "a returned man having enlisted in Winnipeg."

Albert Quickfall. Left this life on February 14, 1935. Age 36 - killed at Island Mt. Mine. "Rest in Peace."

Floyd deWitt Reed. Cariboo Lodge No.4 A.F. & A.M. Born Washington Co. Ohio, U.S.A. 1882 - 1932

Reed was a trapper and guide in partnership with Frank Kibbee for 14 years. A creek on the Bowron Lake chain is named for him.

In memory of James Reed. Died February 10, 1904
A Mason.

Sacred to the memory of Marcos Pares Resendos. Died July 19, 1880. Aged 9 months

Marcos was the son of Albino Resendos, who in the census of 1881 was listed as a 46-year-old Mexican bricklayer.

Ellie Roddick 1870-1948 [see below].

John P. Roddick 1860-1948

Roddick was born in Meanbank, Scotland. He came to Barkerville about 1897. He was a Lowhee mine foreman. John predeceased his wife by 18 days. Ellie Roddick was an Australian who came to Canada as a governess in 1898. For 34 years she pumped out hymns on the St. Saviour's Church organ.

William George Roebottom died in July 1867, killed by a falling tree in Black Jack Gulch. He was an ex-Royal Engineer who worked on the Cariboo Road and ran a sternwheeler on the Fraser. He was born in Leeds, England. Age about 35. He left a wife and three children in Victoria. No marker.

In memory of S.A. Rogers. Our friend. God touched him and he slept. June 4, 1911. Until the day breaks and the shadows fall away. Song of Songs IV:6
Rogers was an Overlander of '62. He was born in Northern Ireland in 1840 and four years later moved with his parents to Canada West. In Cariboo he began a series of businesses, including an express line and a general store. He was sheriff of the Cariboo-Lillooet district for four years, a director of the Royal Cariboo Hospital and was elected to the Legislative Assembly of B.C. as a Conservative in 1890; returned in 1894; defeated in 1898, returned in 1900 and defeated again in 1903. He remained unmarried.

In memory of W.M. Rogers. Born at Godstone, Surrey, Eng. Died September 19th, 1866. Aged 28. Requiescat in Pace

Sacred to the memory of Roland Rowland Native of Carnarvon, Wales. Died 5 August 1872. Age 29
Rowland and Colin Chisholm were crushed to death at the McLaughlin Co. in a hydraulic claim cave-in. Rowland had been here less than a year. Chisholm is buried in the Richfield cemetery.

James Ross. Born Goderich, Ontario. Died April 14, 1927. Aged about 86

In memory of Robt. Ruddell. Late of Halton Co. Ontario. Died 5 Dec. 1867. Aged 34 years
Ruddell had only been in the area two years when he was killed in a snow slide on Grouse Creek.

In memory of Samuel Shoemaker. A native of Pennsylvania, U.S.A. Born 1867 Died October 1, 1896 at Willow River. Aged 29 years

In memory of Samuel Sincock. Died June 10, 1907 aged 83 years

Sincock mined in Grass Valley, California, with partner John Bryant. They headed for the Fraser in '58. Sincock was a saloon keeper and lived on the Lowhee Gulch tailings where the town of Wells is located. He arrived in Victoria from San Francisco in May 1858 with several other English partners.

By 1891 he was operating a saloon on Lowhee Creek, near the present town of Wells.

Albert Smith lies here, his plot unmarked. The *Cariboo Observer* records that he died September 20, 1913. He was an employee of the West Canadian Deep Lead Co. and died of a shooting accident on Mt. Greenburg.

Mrs. Muller used to tell his story to visitors. "Be careful where you walk! John Oswick and Albert Smith are resting there beneath the pathway. We've put a flower bed around them. Really, Smith should not be here at all. Shot himself accidentally one day on Mount Murray. Tied a bootlace around his leg to stop the blood. But it didn't work. The whole town turned out to look for him. He could see us searching, miles below, but could not make us hear."

The newspaper account quotes Dr. Callanan as saying the wound from the 12-gauge shotgun would have resulted in death in 20 minutes.

Sacred to the memory of John Wesley Stevenson, a native of Westfield, New Brunswick. Died Nov. 18, 1873. Aged 26 years 6 months
Stevenson was killed with Edward Kimball when they were both buried in an avalanche. Their stones were erected a year later.

Sacred to the memory of **William Stewart**, a native of Scotland. Died Aug. 1, 1884. Aged 56 years. Erected by his friends

In memory of **Alexander Stobo**. Native of West Boag, Scotland. Died April 29, 1869. Aged 39 years

Stobo hit the Fraser in June 1860 and Cariboo in 1861 and like many other miners died in a mine accident—drowned in the bedrock drain with a fellow Chinese worker when water broke into the Caledonia Claim shaft. Three to four hundred miners stopped digging to gather at the Masonic Hall and pay tribute. The *Cariboo Sentinel* said he was, "a man mourned by all who have been acquainted with him in the Cariboo...though his name may not be handed down to posterity on the tablets of fame his memory will be ever cherished by the circle which had the privilege of calling him friend. Unassuming, cheerful, industrious, and generous, ever ready and anxious to assist a friend to the utmost of his power, he has gone to his long home honoured and lamented." Few could ask for a better epitaph.

Poet James Anderson remembered him and others years after he left Williams Creek when he wrote:

Where are the boys of '63,
When the "boom" was in Cariboo?
The big bully boys of "roaring camp,"
Rough ready boys and true?

The Watties, the Cummings, the Stevenson boys,
The Laidlaw, Jamie and Bill
Thomson, John Bowron, Steele, J. MacLaren,
Stobo and Fraser and Hill!

"Some will return to 'Lochaber no more,"
"Ne'er return to their 'ain countree,"
Peace to the dead! But I ask you where
Are the boys of '63?

In memory of **James Stone** Born Kidderminster, Worcestershire, England. February 10, 1843. Died October 11, 1910

Stone was a telegraph operator in 1891 and was also postmaster from 1880 to 1910. James and Marie Stone (nee Michel) married in about 1880 and had a daughter Elizabeth and son Leslie. When James died Marie married Duncan McIntyre. She is buried here. See McIntyre.

In loving Memory of **Leslie J.D. Stone**. Died January 24, 1907. Age 16 years, 7 months, 5 days

Leslie was the son of James and Mary Stone. See above. Leslie died of typhoid fever. Though only a young lad, Leslie was already doing a man's work and was "the pride and mainstay of his family."

Sacred to the Memory of **Captain O.J. Travaillot**. Late Surveyor - Royal Engineers. Died Royal Cariboo Hospital, Barkerville, B.C. February 2, 1879

Oswald Justice Travaillot was hired on July 13, 1858, as the first Revenue Officer for the district of Fort Dallas or Forks of the Thompson. He resigned early the next year. He later became a B.C. Land Surveyor. See J. B. Malamon.

George. J. Walker. Born Barkerville Dec. 31, 1869. Died March 18, 1912

A Mason. Walker was the son of Samuel Walker, the keeper of the Albion Saloon in Barkerville. Samuel arrived in 1863. There is no record of George's mother, but by 1881 Samuel was a widower. George succeeded John Bowron as Gold Commissioner and Government Agent. He died "of kidney trouble," leaving a wife and two sons.

In memory of **Adam Watson**. Died 10th Oct. 1880. Aged 56 years. A native of Greenock, Scotland

Watson was one Barkerville resident who avoided accidents long enough to die of heart disease.

Sacred to the memory of Mary Webster. Born Worthing, England. Died 29 June 1864. Aged 53 years. May her soul R.I.P.

Mary Ann Webster was one of a handful of women who applied for a mining licence. She was the first into the office on June 22, 1863. She came here with two daughters in 1862, one of whom, Mrs. Cusheon, was active in mining and appears to have run a boarding house with her husband in Cameronton. There is no record indicating if Webster was married or widowed, although several men named Webster were around at that time.

Sacred to the memory of David Whiteford, who departed this life Nov. 10, 1866. Aged 33. Born at Kilwinning, County Ayr, Scotland. By his exemplary character he won the esteem and respect of many sincere friends. Erected by his co-partners in the Reid Claim, Conklins Gulch

Sam Wilcox. Wilcox is buried here, somewhere. He arrived on the creeks in 1863.

Sacred to the memory of J.B. Wilkinson, M.D. Born in Canada. Died November 3, 1869. Aged 35 years. Erected by his Cariboo friends, Nov. 1880

Dr. Wilkinson was born in Eglington, York County, Canada West. He came to B.C. at the beginning of the gold rush, reportedly one of the first to reach Rich Bar at Quesnel. He sought gold but found a desperate need for medical care and returned to his practice. He was the physician of Sophie Cameron, John "Cariboo" Cameron's wife and was one of the men to help pull out the sled with her coffin in the winter of 1863. Dr. Wilkinson died at Richfield after a short illness.

Mrs. William Winnard died suddenly at Barkerville, April 4, 1865. Doctors put it down to heart disease. Two months later a benefit was held to send her children to school in Victoria. In 1868 her husband died. William was a blacksmith, age 53, and he too may be buried in an unmarked plot in this cemetery.

Sacred to the memory of Mary Wintrip. Beloved wife of Edward Wintrip, who departed this life Sept. 2, 1879. Born Northumberland

> *Here perfect bliss can ne'er be found*
> *The honest mind—*
> *Midst changing scenes and dying friends*
> *Be Thou my all in all.*

There are no records of Mary Wintrip other than a note from Lottie Bowron indicating she committed suicide by hanging. Edward Wintrip was a blacksmith in Barkerville. In 1881 Edward, age 52, was living with Lewis Wintrip, 56, Robert, age 58 and his son John, age 22. Edward was listed as a widower. Edward was still there in 1891. Lewis arrived on the creeks in 1863.

In Loving Memory of John C. Wintrip 1855 - 1930

John came to Barkerville in 1870 at age 13 to join his father Robert Wintrip and his uncles. He lived in a cabin at the mouth of Stouts Gulch.

Appendix 2
THE RICHFIELD CEMETERY

The Richfield Cemetery was located just north of the town on a hillside near St. Patrick's Roman Catholic church, built in 1868. The site was used mainly by Catholics and Chinese and, judging by the dates of death, preceded the building of the church. The cemetery was not kept up by Barkerville residents and no restoration has been attempted, so no markers remain. In 1959 there were two: Patrick Fitzpatrick and T. Le Mulard. The Chinese graves were exhumed and the bones sent back to China, a custom ensuring one rested with his ancestors.

This list is compiled mainly from newspapers accounts and includes all those reported as interred at Richfield. Doubtless there were many more, particularly the Chinese whose deaths were seldom reported by the newspapers.

James Barry, murderer of Charles Morgan Blessing. He was hanged at Richfield August 12, 1867, at the same time as Indian Nikel Palsk, also convicted of murder. They were interred "near the burial ground at Richfield."

Michael Carney. The *Cariboo Sentinel,* November 28, 1868, reported that on Tuesday, November 23, 1868, Carney died in Barkerville and was interred in the Roman Catholic cemetery. He was a native of Ireland and a citizen of the U.S. His death was the result of a shaft cave-in.

Colin Chisholm was crushed to death with Roland Rowland July 3, 1872, while working in the McLaughlin Co. hydraulic claim. He was much respected and came to this country from Prince Edward Island. He was about 50 years old.

*In memory of **Patrick Fitzpatrick,** of County Cavan, Ireland, who departed this life on the 15th March, 1868, aged 32 years. Requiescat in pace*

Patrick was not a nice young man, and it may be with some justification that he died an early death. In May 1866 he was arrested for conspiring to swindle C. Wren out of $548.50 at one of the frequent Barkerville horse races. The result was not recorded, but that December Fitzpatrick was again in county court where Patrick Kirwin had taken action to recover a loan of $221.

Michael Hanley, a native of County Tipperary, Ireland, died at the Cariboo Hospital, August 7, 1875, of typhoid fever. He was one of the original shareholders in the Black Bull Co., Lowhee Creek, and had been in the area since 1862.

William Macartney, a native of Ardee township, Cool County, Louth Ireland, aged about 36-40. Macartney fell into the bedrock flume, on the Cornish Co's ground near Richfield.

He had emigrated to the U.S. in 1851 or 52 and then mined in Australia. He moved back to California and mined on French Gulch in the Shasta country. He came to B.C. early in 1858. He was a partner in the Cornish Co.

T. Le Mulard, Born in France, Decease Le 12 Avril, 1869, Age de 44 ans

A *Cariboo Sentinel* obituary says: "Theophile Mullard, a native of the department of Seine et Oise, died

The Cornish Hydraulic Claim on Williams Creek, where William Macartney was killed. PABC #10202

of paralysis on the 12th inst., in the Cariboo Hospital, of which he had been an inmate for the last nine months. The deceased who was 45 years of age was formerly a miner on Nelson Creek. His remains were interred in the cemetery at Richfield on Wednesday, and were followed to the grave by a numerous and respectable concourse of mourners."

Nikel Palsk, a native Indian, was hung for the murder of a miner named Morgan, whom Palsk and a partner murdered on the Cariboo Road in 1867. He was hung with James Barry.

Ah Mow, a Chinese restaurant keeper was stabbed and killed by an assailant, November 3, 1870, in front of his establishment on Barkerville's main street. Jean Boulanger, a native of France, alias John Baker, was charged with murder. Despite being identified by other Chinese, a bloody jacket and a similar knife being found on his person, he was acquitted by the all-white jury.

THE STANLEY CEMETERY

The Stanley Cemetery, located near the almost-vanished town of Stanley, west on Highway 27, is not as well preserved as the Barkerville Cemetery, but there are grave markers of historic interest. In the 1870s Barkerville was in a slump, and many miners and merchants moved, at least temporarily, to the new town of Stanley.

Josiah Crosby Beedy. Born in Pennsylvania, U.S. Died Van Winkle B.C. January 27, 1880

Beedy was a partner in a general store, Beedy and Townsend. The proprietors claimed to "keep on hand everything required in a mining camp." Prior to running this business in Stanley, Beedy tried an experiment in transportation. He brought in two of "R.W. Thompson's Patent Indian Rubber Tire Road Steamers," grotesque pieces of equipment that looked like steam rollers. In a race they were tortoises, slow and steady—that is, until they came to hills. Then they stopped. At the base of Jackass Mountain the Road Steamers ground to a halt, unable to climb the grade. The rusting hulks lay by the roadside for years.

John Evans [indecipherable]

John Evans was the leader of the Company of Welsh Adventurers, a party of 26 men formed in Wales in 1862. They reached Victoria in June 1863 and Lightning Creek late that summer. Their experience in Welsh mines gave them an edge, but Cariboo was a mine of a different color. Members soon began to desert. Within a few years only three remained in Cariboo: John Evans, Harry Jones and Robert F. Pritchard. Evans was elected to the B.C. Legislature and died in office in 1877.

Sacred to the memory of John Greep. Native of Devon, England. Departed this life April —1877, aged 38 years. May he live with God

Harry Jones. Born Carnorvonshire, Wales. September 29, 1840. With the "Welsh Adventurers" arrived in B.C. June 1863. Last survivor of the famous Evans Party and one of Cariboo's best-known and best-loved pioneers. Represented Cariboo in B.C. Legislature 1903-09. Died February 25, 1936. Buried at Stanley, B.C.

Jones returned to Portmadog Wales in 1876, "having made a good deal of money," according to Evans. A decade later he returned to B.C. to mine at Granite Creek. He came back here a year later.

Sacred to the memory of Yoachim Wilhelm Lindhard. Native of Stege Denmark. Died June 9, 1873. Aged 38 years

Lindhard came to Van Winkle in 1865, after operating an express company on the Harrison Lake-Lillooet Trail in 1859. In the early 1870s he opened a meat market in Barkerville. At the burial service Captain John Evans presided, and the *Sentinal* reported, "Not one claim on Lightning Creek worked. Every house and store was closed at an early hour, and remained so until night. Sorrow was depicted on every countenance."

None Gau

Bill Hong in his book *And So— That's How It Happened* says that Wong Man Ding, Cariboo Jack, lived here for 50 years. On his one trip out to Prince George he brought back "a sporting girl named None Gau, but better known as 'old Potatoes.'" She died just

A Chinese funeral in Barkerville. BVHP

before Wong returned to China and is the only Chinese buried in Stanley.

John Peebles. Born in Loghee, Scotland, Oct. 23, 1833. Died Sept. 2, 1889. At Rest

A few years ago, while John Peebles was At Rest, his tombstone was stolen, along with several others from this cemetery. Publicity over the theft resulted in its anonymous return.

Peebles came to Cariboo in 1863, where he was associated in the Murtle Co. claim. He lived in Stanley and pre-empted land at Beaver Pass. John was married to Ellen Dickie Peebles, born 1849. In 1881 they had two children, William, 9, and James D., 5. In the 1881 census he was listed as a blacksmith and storekeeper.

Although the headboard says, Died 1889, John was alive for the 1891 census. Lot 408 at Beaver Pass was in his name in 1899, but lot 407, Henry Georgeson's, was Crown granted to Ellen in August 1901.

Robert F. Pritchard

Many of the graves in the Stanley cemetery are no longer marked, the headboards stolen, weathered and crumbled. Robert Pritchard was the blacksmith of the Welsh Adventurers and was one of three who stayed in Cariboo. He signed on at Portmadog, Wales. Pritchard died in 1915 and is known to have been buried here, but his marker is gone. The 1881 census lists him as 44 years old.

In memory of E. Schuetzy. Aged 43 years. Died May 6, 1875

Abe Stott. Born January 19, 1870. Rochdale, Lancashire, England. Died July 22, 1926

Stott was a window dresser, a man with an unlikely trade for the gold-fields. Stott and his friend Patrick McKenna, buried in Cameronton, discovered gold on Eight Mile Creek while on a fishing trip. He was also a partner with John Oswick.

FRIENDS OF BARKERVILLE AND CARIBOO GOLDFIELDS HISTORICAL SOCIETY

On July 9, 1985, in a small cabin in Wells, a group of Wellsites, Barkervillians and summer residents met to discuss the need for a society that would act as a lobby group for historical and environmental concerns as they affected the goldfields. They identified the need for conservation funding; to locate and reopen historic trails; funding for publication programs and research projects; and a lobby group on behalf of Barkerville.

Present at the first historic meeting were Kevin Brown, Ron Candy, Arden Craig, Eva Grandell, Sue Smith, Ron Young and Richard Wright, from which came the first executive.

That first meeting defined the areas of concern as the Cariboo goldfields, centering on Barkerville. A later project-oriented public meeting identified trails, a telegraph line, archeology, publications and a heritage inventory of the area as primary projects.

Since that time the Friends society has taken on and completed a variety of projects. These include: a report, site clearing, basic building stabilization and As-Found drawings of the Quesnelle Forks townsite; the clearing of the Stanley-Richfield Cariboo Wagon Road trail; the locating and construction of the Barkerville View Trail; database compilations of land and mining records; archives cataloging for Barkerville Historic Townsite; costume construction; archival research; ski trails and shelter construction; cemetery restoration; trail marking and research in the goldfields area; construction of the Gunn and Canadian claims displays on Williams Creek, and various upkeeping and landscaping projects in Barkerville and Wells. In addition, it has acted as a spokesperson and lobbyist for the historic aspects of Barkerville on several government studies and task forces.

The work of the Friends, recently enlarged to take in the mandate of the old Cariboo Historical Society with the name Friends of Barkerville and Cariboo Goldfields Historical Society, continues with a diversity of projects. The group actively seeks new members, volunteers as well as private and corporate sponsors for displays and projects. Anyone interested in joining the group or offering sponsorship should contact:

The Friends of Barkerville and Cariboo Goldfields Society
c/o Barkerville Historic Townsite
Barkerville, B.C. V0K 1B0

Databases and research compiled by Friends of Barkerville are helping historians remove layers of mystery and doubt from Cariboo history. This photo, for instance, was once thought to be Billy Barker. In fact, it is John King Barker, a founder of the Bullion Pit near Quesnelle Forks. Beside him is a $135,000 gold brick.

Quesnelleforks, seen here in the 1960s, has been the site of major projects by Friends of Barkerville.

Selected Bibliography

Anonymous. *Cariboo Lodge. Spanning a Century with Freemasons of Cariboo*. Cariboo Observer, Quesnel.

Anderson, James. *Sawney's Letters and Cariboo Rhymes*. Barkerville Restoration and Advisory Committee.

Bancroft, H.H. *History of British Columbia*. San Francisco: The History Company, 1887.

Beeson, Edith. *Dunleavy: From the Diaries of Alex P. McInnes*. Lillooet, B.C.: Lillooet Publishers, 1971.

Cheadle, Walter B. *Cheadle's Journal of a Trip Across Canada 1862-1863*. Edmonton: Hurtig, 1971.

Elliott, R. Gordon. *Barkerville, Quesnel & the Cariboo Gold Rush*. Vancouver: Douglas & McIntyre, 1980.

Hong, W.M. *...And So... That's How It Happened*. Quesnel, B.C.: W.M. Hong, 1978.

Howay, F.W., and Scholefield, E.O.S. *British Columbia from the Earliest Times to the Present*. Vancouver: Clarke, 1914.

Lindsay, F.W. *Cariboo Dreams*. Lumbey, B.C.: Lindsay, 1971.

_____ *Cariboo Yarns*. Quesnel, B.C.: Lindsay, 1962.

Ludditt, Fred W. *Barkerville Days*. Langley, B.C.: Mr. Paperback, 1980.

_____ *Gold in the Cariboo*. Courtenay, B.C.: E.W. Bickle, 1978.

_____ *Campfire Sketches of the Cariboo*. Penticton, B.C.: Ludditt, 1974.

Ormsby, Margaret A. *British Columbia: A History*. Toronto: Macmillan, 1958.

Ramsey, Bruce. *Barkerville*. Vancouver: Mitchell Press.

Skelton, Robin. *They Call it the Cariboo*. Victoria: Sono Nis Press, 1982.

Walkem, W. Wymond, M.D. *Stories of Early British Columbia*. Vancouver: News-Advertiser, 1914.

Weir, Joan. *Canada's Gold Rush Church*. Anglican Diocese of Cariboo.

Williams, David Ricardo. *The Man for a New Country: Sir Matthew Baillie Begbie*. Sidney, B.C.: Gray's Publishing, 1977.

Wright, Richard Thomas. *Bowron Lakes: A Year-round Guide*. Surrey, B.C.: Heritage Publishing Co., 1985.

_____ *In a Strange Land: A Pictorial Record of the Chinese in Canada 1788-1923*. Saskatoon, Sask.: Western Prod. Prairie Books, 1988.

_____ *Overlanders*. Saskatoon, Sask.: Western Producer Prairie Books, 1985.

INDEX

172

173

174

About the Author

This book by writer Richard Thomas Wright combines the author's established talent for writing with his love of Canadian history.

Well known as an historical writer and photographer, Wright has explored much of this province and its history by canoe, on cross-country skis and by foot, and has spent many summers and a few winters in gold rush country. For several years Wright was an historical interpreter in Barkerville, creating the character of James Kelso.

He has had 22 books published, including *The Overlanders,* the story of the westward Canadian movement to the gold fields of British Columbia, and *In a Strange Land,* a pictorial history of the Chinese in Canada. He has written over 500 magazine articles and is an award-winning newspaper columnist.

Wright worked as a journalist for several years, first with the *Quesnel Cariboo Observer,* then as managing editor of the *Cowichan News Leader* in Duncan, B.C. and as a locum editor for Cariboo Press.

He now lives at Pioneer Ranch near Williams Lake in the Cariboo, where he and his wife Cathryn Wellner operate the ranch, tour as atorytellers and are partners in GrassRoots Consulting Group Inc., a communications and economic development company.

Richard was the recipient of a BC Heritage Trust Award of Recognition in 1996, for "an outstanding commitment to the heritage of British Columbia" and was appointed to the BC Heritage Trust board of directors in 1998.

Richard and Cathryn are currently working on two more books on the Cariboo goldfields. *The Great Cariboo Wagon Road* is a mile-by-mile guide to history along the Cariboo Wagon Road. The second, *Whiskey Dealers and Fallen Angels,* will look at the women who populated the gold creeks. They are also producing a series of CD's on the early music of the gold fields and British Columbia.

Website: http/grassrootsgroup.com